COLONIAL ST. LOUIS

COLONIAL
ST. LOUIS

BUILDING A CREOLE CAPITAL

CHARLES E. PETERSON, FAIA

THE PATRICE PRESS
TUCSON, ARIZONA

Second Printing—April 2001

ISBN 1-880397-43-9 $14.95

Published by
The Patrice Press
Box 85639 ☐ Tucson AZ 85754-5639
Toll-free: 1/800/367-9242
Email: books@patricepress.com
Website: http://patricepress.com

Printed in the United States of America

To the memory of Charles van Ravenswaay
Joe Desloge, Arthur Hoskins, John Francis McDermott
John Albury Bryan, and other members of the
William Clark Society,
who enlivened the historical scene in St. Louis,
and to Irving Dilliard, who, happily, is still with us.

CONTENTS

Preface to the First Edition

In the nineteenth century a modern city completely grew over the old town of St. Louis and its plow lands. Except for the pattern of the streets we will not find a single landmark of the early period. Even the Mississippi itself has been so changed that the first settlers would no longer know it. It is the literary task of this essay to provide an eighteenth century view of the Creole settlement which was the capital of Upper Louisiana. To learn of its nature we must go to the surviving documents. Fortunately, there are many of them.

In the period of 1936-41 a great quantity of basic historical data was collected by National Park Service architects in making a study of the riverfront area of the Jefferson National Expansion Memorial. This great project embraces the largest part of the old town site. Part of the collection was assembled in 1938-40. In its direction I was assisted by G. Vietor Davis and Herbert L. Moscowitz. A large part of the data used in this essay was thus made available in convenient form.

McCune Gill, vice-president of the Title Insurance Corporation of St. Louis and expert in the history of real estate, has been extremely helpful by guiding me to the land records and by making the collections of his company available. The staff of the Missouri Historical Society, especially the late Nettie Beauregard, the late Stella Drumm Atkinson, Marjory Douglas, and Brenda Gieseker, have given ready cooperation over a period of twelve years.

It is to be hoped that the many thousands of official manuscripts relating to this period known to exist in the archives of Seville and other depositories will soon be published, for our present knowledge of St. Louis in its frontier days is far from complete. The program of the St. Louis Historical Documents Foundation, beginning with the Nasatir collection in San Diego, may be expected to contribute materially.

This work is reprinted from installments appearing in the issues of the *Missouri Historical Society Bulletin* for April, July, and October, 1947, with corrections and additions, including illustrations.

Charles E. Peterson

PREFACE TO THE SECOND EDITION

FOR NOW MY LITTLE BOOK on St. Louis, written so many years ago, will have to stand as first published by the Missouri Historical Society. But we are taking the opportunity of adding some illustrations collected since then. And, in particular, a detailed description of Laclède's base at the village of New Chartres. From it St. Louis was founded, sixty miles upriver, in February 1764.

The story has been told many times of how the founding party from New Orleans reached the Illinois Country in November 1763. But only now have we learned that Laclède actually bought a substantial property near the new stone fort on the east bank of the Mississippi. There he had snug quarters for the winter and provisions to send up the river to the new townsite.

Laclède's purchase was recorded by the notary Labuxiére on November 19, as follows:

> Was present in person Jean Gerardin, private in the troops detached of the Marine, garrisoned in Illinois, residing in new Chartres, who by the presents has acknowledged and confesses to have on this day, sold, ceded, quitted and conveyed, and promises to warrant against all troubles, debts, dowers, mortgages, evictions, substitutions and all other incumbrances whichever generally, unto Messrs. Maxant, Laclède and Co., merchants, residing commonly in New Orleans, said Mr. Laclède being presently in Illinois, here present and accepting acquirer for himself, and Messrs. Maxant and Co., to wit: one house built on sills, consisting in two rooms, two closets, a shed, the lot belonging to said house, of which the parties cannot tell the dimensions, and on which there is a barn covered with straw, a pigeon house, a well of wood and other conveniences; said lot enclosed with cedar posts on all its faces . . . the whole situate in New Chartres, and further all the furniture now in said house of whatever description they may be, and of which the parties have not thought proper to make a more ample statement, further seventeen head of cattle, one thousand weight of tobacco, twenty hogs, one hundred and fifty fowls, and such as the whole now stands and lies in which said Mr. Laclède says he well knows for having seen and visited the same, without reserving or retaining anything on the part of said Girardin . . .

This notable document surfaced in *The Village of Chartres in Colonial Illinois, 1720-1765* by Margaret Kimball Brown and Lawrie Cena Dean (New Orleans: Polyanthos Press, 1977, 788-90).

Charles E. Peterson
Society Hill, Philadelphia
July 1992

COLONIAL ST. LOUIS

COLONIAL ST. LOUIS

S<small>T. LOUIS, FOUNDED IN</small> 1764, had an early background remote from
the English settlements on the Atlantic Seaboard. Like Detroit and New
Orleans, it was established by the rival French and had grown to some
importance before the great migration crossed the Appalachians.

Life in the Creole villages of the "Illinois Country" had a special flavor
of its own. Canadians settled there at the end of the seventeenth century and other French from the Louisiana coast and Europe were soon
to join them. The friendliness of the Indians and the abounding fertility of the countryside enabled these people to live comfortably in the
wilderness and a century more or less was to pass before they were rudely
jostled into the modern world.[1] St. Louis, the largest and most impor-

---

1. The founding of Cahokia, the first white settlement on the Mississippi River, is considered
as the establishment of the mission to the Tamaroa Indians by priests from the Seminary of Quebec
in 1699. An expedition left Quebec the preceding summer, arrived at the site of the proposed
mission in December, and passed on to the Arkansas country. That winter, Father Jean François
Buisson de St. Cosme, one of the first party, returned to the Tamaroa Indians and set about erecting a chapel. This was opened and the mission cross raised in the third week of May 1699. Gilbert
J. Garraghan, S.J., "New Light on Old Cahokia," *Illinois Catholic Historical Review,* 11 (October
1928): 99-146. The village prospered until St. Louis was founded, but declined thereafter under
English and American domination. Plans are being formulated to celebrate in 1949 the 250th an-
niversary of this important date in Mississippi Valley history.

In what is now the state of Missouri, St. Louis was antedated by several temporary establishments,
including the Jesuit mission on the River des Peres (1700), Bourgmond's fort on the Missouri
River (1723) and a number of lead mining camps of which Mine la Motte (c. 1722) was possibly
the first. Ste. Genevieve, established across from Kaskaskia on the west side of the Mississippi
about the middle of the eighteenth century, had to be moved on account of floods. The town on

tant of these villages, was forty years old before it became an American possession. Its *habitants* spoke, dressed and thought differently. They drank *tafia*, paddled *pirogues*, followed wheeled plows and built a different kind of house. The voyageur, the Indian, and the farmer mingled in the streets of this diminutive frontier capital which newcomers from the East found curious indeed.

The establishment of St. Louis was an operation of the New Orleans firm of Maxent, Laclède and Company which, in 1763, was granted a monopoly of the rich Indian fur trade of the Upper Missouri country.[2] Pierre Laclède Liguest, one of the partners, left New Orleans in August of that year for the long voyage up the Mississippi. In November he arrived at Fort de Chartres and spent the winter there. This gave him time to scout out a good site for his new post, get acquainted with the local Canadian French who were to become its inhabitants, and secure workmen for its construction. After exploring as far as the mouth of the Missouri, a location was selected. When navigation opened up, a party of thirty men, "nearly all mechanics," landed at the site of St. Louis, began to clear it of trees, and put up temporary shelter for men, tools and provisions.[3] This was on February 14, 1764.

Few founders in American history made as wise a choice of sites as

---

its present site is a generation younger than St. Louis.

On the east side of the river the rich lowlands (known from the Spanish period as the "American Bottom") supported a small but flourishing agriculture. This in turn sustained the fur traders, lead miners, and garrisons of the upper valley and provided convoys of grain for the new and sometimes starving settlements of the Gulf Coast. All of this vast territory on both sides of the river, first developed and dominated by the French, was known both officially and popularly as the "Illinois Country."

European politics caused a drastic shift in the local scene and after the Seven Years War and the treaties of Fontainebleau and Paris, England came to own the east side of the Mississippi and Spain the west. St. Louis was founded just at this time.

For a picture of life on the left bank of the Mississippi, see Clarence W. Alvord, *The Illinois Country, 1673-1818* (Springfield, 1920); Joseph H. Schlarmann, *From Quebec to New Orleans* (Belleville, Ill. 1929); and Natalia Maree Belting "The French Villages of the Illinois Country," in *The Canadian Historical Review* (March 1943). For Ste. Genevieve see Ward A. Dorrance, "The Survival of French in the Old District of Ste. Genevieve," *University of Missouri Studies* 10 (1935). The correct use of the word "Creole" is defined in Dorrance, 5, and in John Francis McDermott, *A Glossary of Mississippi Valley French, 1673-1850* (St. Louis, 1941).

2. John Francis McDermott, "The Exclusive Trade Privilege of Maxent, Laclede and Company," *Missouri Historical Review*, 29 (1935).

3. Hunt's Minutes (H. Min.), (typescript at Missouri Historical Society), April 18, 1825. Auguste Chouteau, "Journal of the Founding of St. Louis," *Missouri Historical Society Collections*, 3: 335-66. A temporary warehouse on the river's edge was one of the first buildings built. H. Min., Nov. 16, 1825, 4 (St. Louis, 1911), 349-66. This was a sketch based on memory many years afterwards. Laclède kept a journal, as McDermott points out, but it has been lost. Of the numerous reports and other documents which must have been filed in connection with the founding and first growth of St. Louis, none is now available.

did Laclède for his *Poste de St. Louis.* Topographically, it occupied the first elevated site below the meeting of the three great river routes—the Mississippi, the Missouri, and the Illinois—against which boats could be landed. Strategically, it stood directly between his English rivals and the rich fur trade of the Missouri River. The site was a gently sloping plateau with good drainage for building sites and no deep ravines to embarrass the building of streets. The site was very heavily timbered[4] and thus well provided with firewood and lumber in the raw. Durable building stone outcropped in abundance. It was geographically remote from any potential enemy of strength. Laclede was so pleased with the place that he believed his settlement might become "one of the finest cities in America."[5]

By early June 1764 there were two or three temporary huts with many of the population living on platforms six or seven feet high "to protect themselves from wild beasts." Priority was given the construction of the large stone building for the company headquarters[6] though progress was embarrassed by the arrival of a friendly but thievish tribe of Missouri Indians who wanted to give up their wild ways and become a suburb of the new post. They were eventually persuaded to leave and those citizens who had fled across the river returned to their work.[7]

The outline of the founder's plan was soon to be filled in. The only population available was in the old French villages across the river and Laclède spared no means to attract it to his new settlement. The propaganda created for the purpose[8] was so effective that several places were nearly depopulated. Although the ferries were guarded to stop them, emigrants crossed the river by night, even carrying doors, windows, and other parts of their dwellings with them. Few of the French wanted to stay behind and take their chances under English rule on the east bank. Consequently, St. Louis was never a lone cabin in a clearing; it was a commercial place with money behind it and flourished from the very beginning.

The success of the new trading establishment was even admitted by the rival British. Captain Harry Gordon noted in his journal for August 31, 1766:

---

4. H. Min., July 29, 1825. Testimony of Baptiste Riviere.
5. Chouteau, 352.
6. Wilson Primm, "History of St. Louis," Missouri Historical Society Collections, 4 (1913): 167.
7. Chouteau, 353.
8. Farmar to Gage, Dec. 16-19, 1765. Illinois State Historical Society Collections, 11: 130. At the time there was no communication with the Atlantic seaboard; Detroit and New Orleans were the closest places of importance on the French lines of travel.

The village of Paint Court [St. Louis]⁹ is pleasantly situated on a high Ground which forms the W. Bank of the Mississipi, it is 3 miles higher up than Kyahokie [Cahokia]—has already fifty Families supported chiefly from thence, & seems to flourish very quick.

At This Place Mr. Le Clef [Laclède] the principal Indian Trader resides, who takes so good Measures, that the whole Trade of the Missouri That of the Mississipi Northwards, and that of the Nations near la Baye, Lake Michigan, and St. Josephs, by the Illinois River, is entirely brought to Him. He appears to be sensible, clever, & has been very well educated; is very active, and will give us some Trouble before we get the Parts of this Trade that belong to us out of His Hands.¹⁰

Whether or not Laclède originally intended to found a village is not known. A concentration of farmers and artisans near his trading establishment would bring the benefits of a home-grown food supply, defense by a local militia and other advantages. It would also give him an opportunity to keep his eye on rival traders. He was evidently not satisfied with the existing settlements which had been first located near the Indians in the bottomlands and were often flooded. In any case he quickly contrived an admirable plan for a new village. This continued the land use traditions of the older French villages (as promised) and introduced the logic and regularity of the Spanish colonial town-building policies.¹¹

The Spanish, having settled the vast territory from Mexico to Chile, were veterans at this sort of thing and had regulations to cover all contingencies. It is interesting to note how closely Laclede conformed to Philip II's directives. The law of 1573 directed the prospective founder to select ''an elevated place, where are to be found health, strength, fertility, and abundance of land for farming and pasturage, fuel and wood for building, fresh water [and] a native people. . . .''

Having made sure of the acquiescence of the natives the town should be planned systematically with a commons ''for recreation and for the cattle to be pastured'' and the rest of the adjoining lands laid out for

9. *"Pain Court,"* meaning ''short of bread,'' was a characteristic nickname of the Illinois Country French. Primm, 166. Similarly Carondelet was called *"Vide Poche,"* (empty pockets,) and Ste. Genevieve *"Misère"* (miserable).

10. ''Captain Harry Gordon's Journal'' in Illinois Historical Collections, 11: 299. The British Army engineer Phillip Pittman, who was in the Illinois Country from December 1765 to the spring of 1767, reported at St. Louis ''about forty private houses and as many families.'' Captain Phillip Pittman, *The Present State of the European Settlements on the Mississippi,* London, 1770. Reprinted Cleveland, 1906, 94.

11. Whether or not Laclède at the time knew that St. Louis was on Spanish soil has not been determined. When he left New Orleans the treaty of transfer was nominally secret.

cultivation and distributed in proportion to the number of town lots.[12]

All of these things Laclède did. When Don Pedro Piernas, the first Spanish lieutenant governor, arrived at St. Louis in 1770, he found the main features of the master plan already in execution over an area of some twenty-four square miles.

---

12. The laws, translated by Zelia Nuttal, were reprinted in *Planning and Civic Comment,* 5: 17-20.

THE VILLAGE

FOR REASONS OF SECURITY and sociability nearly all of the Illinois Country *habitants* lived in villages. As Volney wrote:

> Neighbors pay and return visits: for visiting and talking are so indispensably necessary to a Frenchman from habit, that throughout the whole frontier of Canada and Louisiana there is not one settler of that nation to be found, whose house is not within reach or within sight of some other. [1]

Outlying farmhouses were exceptional. The farmer lived alongside the artisan in St. Louis, and their houses formed a compact residential block distinctly separated from the pastures and the cultivated fields. In this respect it resembled many of the old villages of Europe.

Laclède's settlement was given a simple gridiron layout which followed the old custom in Spanish-American town planning. [2] It was a pattern used as far back as the Egyptians, although new to the Illinois Country. French New Orleans, planned by the military engineer de Pauger about 1722, may also have inspired it. Both it and St. Louis had the gridiron plan with a public plaza centered on the riverfront and the dimensions

---

1. C. E. Voleny, *View of the Climate and Soil of the United States of America* (London, 1804), 384.

2. For example, in 1540 Santiago del Nuevo Extremo, in Chile, was laid out in square blocks of four lots each. Helen Douglas Irvine, "The Landholding System of Colonial Chile" in *Hispanic American Historical Review*, 8 (November 1928): 466, 468.

of the streets and the blocks *(isles)* were remarkably similar.[3]

The most accessible landing place for boats determined the location of the public square and this in turn became the center of the town.[4] It was laid out to be a public market place *(marché public)* and was used for the meetings of the militia and public gatherings. The records call it the *"Place Publique,"* the *"Place d'Armes"* or simply *"la Place."* It was first intended to reserve a strip of land 300 feet wide all along the river but this idea changed and the space was granted to individuals for private building lots.[5] In order that all might live close to the river, from which the water supply was drawn, the village was laid out three streets deep, extending up and down the river for some distance.

The three long streets parallel to the river were thirty-six French feet wide.[6] The first and most important bounded *la Place;* it was usually called *La Rue Principale, La Grand Rue,* or *La Rue Royale.*[7] The next street

---

3. The New Orleans blocks were 300 French feet on a side and the streets thirty-two feet wide. U.S. Congress, *American State Papers (ASP)*, Washington, 1832-61, Miscellaneous, I: 348.

In this connection it is interesting to note the official instructions issued for the founding of a settlement at the fort "El Principe de Asturias, Senior Don Carlos" near the mouth of the Missouri River in 1767 and only a few miles from St. Louis. This was the first town building project of the Spanish government in Upper Louisiana. Included in the elaborate orders prepared at New Orleans were the following prescriptions: "The endeavor shall be made to assign the land in perfect squares which will avoid many suits at law and quarrels in the future . . . Between every two lots there shall be a royal (or public) road 12 *varas* wide (roughly 34 feet) and straight." Louis Houck, ed., *The Spanish Regime in Missouri (Sp. Reg.)* (Chicago, 1909), I:10. While this settlement never came into existence, these rules show what the Spanish themselves had in mind for towns in this region.

It is a fact that all the towns founded in Missouri during the Spanish period were of the gridiron type with 300 foot blocks. Even old Ste. Genevieve, moving to a new site about 1784-85, changed to the new order. Mine à Breton, now Potosi, Missouri, was an exception, but its character as a crude mining camp in a valley bottom would explain why it was not laid out with a regular plan.

4. Philip II's law directed that towns be laid out beginning with an oblong plaza not less than 200' x 300' at the landing place.

The St. Louis *Place* was maintained for the most part intact during the colonial period. An exception was the granting of a section 60' x 150' to Benito Vasquez in 1773. *"Livres terreins" (LT)*, III: Fo. 4. MS, Missouri Historical Society. Buenaventura Collel also came to own some of it, but the petition of Madame Loisel, the village midwife, for another section was turned down. The tract became the "Market Place" of the American period; the first market house was built on it in 1811. The last section owned by the public was sold off in 1856. See G. Victor Davis "Notes on Block Seven. The Disappearance of St. Louis' "Place Publique." Typescript, National Park Service, St. Louis, February, 1939.

5. "Memorial," June 30, 1808. Testimony of Delassus, LeDuc and Wherry, H. Min., Nov. 9, 1825. Testimony of Delassus and Auguste Chouteau Nov. 16, 1825. Chouteau, 352. On Sept. 3, 1773, Lieutenant Governor Piernas granted the south part of the square to Benito Vasquez (LT, III: Fo. 4) but the remainder stayed in public ownership for many years. The local militia was an active organization and presumably the area was kept clear, but there are no records of any improvements made on the grounds.

6. The foot as used in the records is the old French foot equaling 12.7893 English inches.

7. Main or First Street in the American period.

up the hill was *Le Rue de L'Eglise,* named after the church.[8] The barns on the hill gave the name to the third and last, *La Rue des Granges.*[9] Crossing these at regular intervals were short thirty-foot-wide streets. In documents involving real estate these are usually referred to simply as *"rues de traverse,"* (cross streets) although some of them had individual names such as *Rue de la Tour,*[10] *Rue de la Place,*[11] *Rue Missouri,*[12] and *Rue Quicapou.*[13] Of these, only the *Rue de la Place* descended to the tow path and landing place on the river.[14]

Of waterfront conditions in this period we know very little. The village was separated from the river by limestone ledges which increased in height toward the north. High water came to the foot of the bluff. At other times the shoreline retreated a considerable distance leaving exposed a wide beach or sand flat. What kind of shipyard was available for building boats and securing them with their gear is not indicated. In two late documents there is mentioned a *"porte"* at St. Louis: The Cerré estate inventory lists two boats and a barge there in 1805 and the Joseph Robidoux estate included three barges, two canoes, one *pirogue,* and a fastening chain at the same place in 1809.[15]

A regular system of blocks was created by the intersecting streets. The important central group of three planned for *La Place,* the company headquarters and the church were 300 feet square. The other blocks were ordinarily 240' x 300'. Subdivision of these into four equal parts was usual, making the typical St. Louis house lot a quarter block of 120' x 150'.[16]

The company headquarters block[17] and the church block adjoining it[18] were set aside at the very beginning. Grants of land were soon made

---

8. Sometimes referred to as *"la deuxième grande rue;"* later, Second Street.

9. Occasionally called *"Rue Barrère,"* after a baker who lived on it; later, Third Street.

10. Walnut Street, named for the tower San Carlos on the hill, built in 1780.

11. Market Street, also called *"Rue Bonhomme."*

12. Chestnut Street.

13. (Kickapoo), Pine Street.

14. Traffic on St. Louis streets included a number of kinds of wheeled vehicles of which the *charette* seems to have been the most common. The streets were not paved and probably little was done to maintain them. A public meeting was held March 15, 1778, at which a committee was appointed to plan and have constructed a drainage ditch along what is now Chestnut Street. Frederic L. Billon, *Annals of St. Louis in Its Early Days* (St. Louis, 1886), 140, 141.

15. St. Louis Recorded Archives (StLRA), 6/1-124.

16. With the passing of years these lots were sometimes divided or added to, causing the pattern of ownership to become increasingly irregular.

17. Confirmation of title recorded Aug. 11, 1766, LT I: Fo. 4.

18. Testimony of Baptiste Riviere, H. Min., Nov. 26, 1825. The site is mentioned as reserved for this purpose in 1766. LT I: Fo. 4. The date of the building of the first church is usually given as 1770, although in 1768 we find mention of *"une grande Rue allant a la chapelle,"* LT. I: Fo. 16. Perhaps this chapel was a tent. Billon, 77. The cemetery on the same block is mentioned as early as 1769, LT I: Fo. 23.

to private individuals. For two years they were assigned by word of mouth, but it evidently was an orderly process without later misunderstandings. In 1766 and afterwards they were recorded in a series of volumes called the *Livres Terreins* or Land Books.[19] These grants include both building sites in the village and in the farm lands outside. The first folio begins with a concession to Joseph Labuscière, the village notary, of *"un Terrein convenable* to set him up in this Post'' between *La Grande Rue* and the river.[20] A double lot (240' x 150') is then awarded to Joseph Calvé, together with a strip of farmland on St. Louis Prairie.[21] These are followed by a grant of a building lot *(un emplacement)* to Jean M. Thoulouze.[22] Francois Bissonet got two standard-size lots in the town as well as land in the Prairie St. Louis and the Grande Prairie.[23] And so on. The general idea was to keep each citizen's holdings in the village and in the fields in proportion.[24]

Such grants were given freely, without charge, in the interest of building up the village. They often contained a clause by which they would revert to the Royal Domain unless developed within a year and a day, and a number were forfeited on that basis. Special uses for the land were mentioned in some cases—as in the grant to Deshetre and Lecompte, who wished to set up a horse mill in partnership[25]—and to Antoine Hubert a 152-foot square "suitable for building a barn to store his grain and for erecting other utilitarian structures.''[26] Once established, titles could be bought, exchanged or mortgaged, and there was a lively turnover in real estate. Land, however, was plentiful and when lots were

---

19. These documents were signed by St. Ange, the provisional commandant of the post, and Judge Lefebvre in lieu of regular Spanish administration, which did not begin until 1770.

20. LT I: Fo. 1. April 1, 1766. No size given.

21. LT I: Fo. 1. Joseph Calvé was an employee of a Ste. Genevieve firm of fur traders. He built a house sixteen feet square on the lot which was sold for debt at a public auction on Sept. 26, 1768, for 600 *livres*. Billon, 50, 59. In 1780 he was one of the enemy leaders in the attack on St. Louis.

22. LT I: Fo. 1. May 1, 1766.

23. LT I: Fo. 1 May 30, 1766. Some form of surveying was done at all times during this period. Auguste Chouteau evidently carried the chain in 1764. Primm, 167. Martin Duralde was also one of the first. He had come up the Mississippi in 1767 with the Rui expedition to which he was attached as general secretary and supervisor *(sobrestante)* at an annual salary of one hundred *pesos*. Jacqueline Trenfel-Treantafeles, "Spanish Occupation of the Upper Mississippi Valley, 1765-1770," (M.A. thesis, Berkeley, Calif., 1941), 97. He was appointed official surveyor of Upper Louisiana by Piernas in 1770. Billon, 57, 447. Antonie Soulard was appointed "Surveyor general for Upper Louisiana" in 1795. Amos Stoddard, *Sketches, Historical and Descriptive of Louisiana* (Philadelphia, 1812), 248. Errors in the original surveys sometimes caused arguments between neighbors at a later day.

24. John Bradbury, *Travels in the Interior of America in the Years 1809, 1810 and 1811.* Reprinted in R. G. Thwaites, Ed., *Early Western Travels* (Cleveland, 1904), 5: 259.

25. LT I: Fo. 2 (June 30, 1766).

26. LT I: Fo. 23 (Feb. 7, 1769).

sold or mortgaged the price was usually determined by the value of improvements. [27]

These building lots seem to have been granted contiguous to each other with the idea of avoiding vacant properties and keeping the village compact for purposes of security. [28] It was customary for each owner to enclose his lot with palisades, called at the time *"pieux en terre"* (stakes in earth) or *"pieux debout"* (stakes upright). This was an old practice among the French in the Mississippi Valley. When New Orleans was laid out it was ordered that all of the property holders "must have their houses or land enclosed by palisades within two months or else they will be deprived of their property and it will revert to the company. . . ."[29] A similar practice was followed in the early villages of the upper Mississippi, including Kaskaskia and Ste. Genevieve. [30] The advantage of having all the private lots enclosed is obvious. By merely barricading the ends of the streets in an emergency it would be possible to have a continuous enclosure all around the village for defense. In any case fences were needed to keep out domestic animals and, being hard to climb, they afforded a measure of privacy and of discouragement to visiting Indians who were often drunk and troublesome. While the enclosure of individual lots is not positively known to have been compulsory at St. Louis, it was required by the 1767 instructions for establishing the settlement at the mouth of the Missouri:

> Outside the houses must run an encircling pointed fence, which will be constructed by each owner at his own expense, in order to prevent

---

27. One unimproved half-lot in the early days was traded for a heifer and a pair of cartwheels. Billon, 152. According to Auguste Chouteau the land was originally owned by the Illinois Indians. (H. Min., Apr. 18, 1825). How the Indian title to the land was extinguished or what specific authority Laclède or St. Ange had to make grants is not known. In the records they make references to "the authority accorded us by the Governors and Intendents of Louisiana." (For example, LT I: Fo. 3, July 4, 1766.)

28. The Spanish idea on this was promulgated in a regulation by Governor Gayoso de Lemos at New Orleans, September, 1797:

> It shall not be permitted to any new settler to form an establishment at a distance from other settlers. The grants of land must be so made as not to have pieces of vacant ground between one and another, since this would offer a greater exposure to the attacks of the Indians, and render more difficult the administration of justice and the regulation of the police, so necessary in all societies, and more particularly in new settlements.

ASP: Public Lands (PL), 4: 5.

29. Sept. 20, 1722. From the "Journal of Diron d'Artaguiette," in Newton C. Mereness, Ed., *Travels in the American Colonies* (New York, 1916), 26.

30. Henry M. Brackenridge describes the enclosure of the Beauvais house in eighteenth century Ste. Genevieve: "The yard was inclosed with cedar pickets, eight or ten inches in diameter, and seven feet high, placed upright, sharpened at the top in the manner of a stockade fort. *Recollections and Places in the West,* 2nd Ed. (Philadelphia, 1868), 21.

the savages from making any sudden rush at night and surprising them.[31]

The stockades were preferably made of mulberry or cedar palisades, but oak and other woods were also used. There was also in use the channeled post *(poteau canellé)* fence usually of mulberry posts and cottonwood boards.[32] Several of the more pretentious residences were surrounded by stone walls, sometimes with loopholes for defense. The records make it clear that these enclosures were used until the end of the colonial period, though not always maintained in good condition.

These generous-sized private enclosures were in some cases divided into a court *(court)* and a garden *(jardin)*. Presumably the former was an area used by domestic animals and poultry and for locking up vehicles and other property as in rural France. The householders paid great attention to gardening and had a good assortment of vegetables. *Caveaux,* or root cellars, were used for the storage of surplus. Orchards were planted in the earliest years and apples and peaches helped to vary the village diet.[33] All in all, the average St. Louisan then enjoyed more space, greenery and privacy at home than at any time since.[34]

As early as 1768 the *"Coteau des Granges"* had its name.[35] The "Hill of Barns" was the rise of ground between the village and the fields of the St. Louis prairie. Many barns were built there,[36] especially in the beginning, on lands acquired just for that purpose. These lots were usually between sixty and eighty feet square[37] and enclosed with fences. The barns were used for sheltering horses and cattle and for storing hay and grain. From them the animals were driven to the commons for pasture.

---

31. Houck, *Sp. Reg.,* I: 16.

32. A contract for one of these in 1770 shows that it was to be four and one-half feet high and made of mulberry posts seven inches thick at the small end. The posts were to be set two and one-half feet in the ground, five feet apart, and channeled or grooved to receive boards of cottonwood. (STLRA, 2/1/85-86). Cedar and oak posts were also used in this unusual type of fence. The fence posts *"a coulisse"* occasionally mentioned seem to have been the same as the post *"canelle."* It was also found in Ste. Genevieve. Ste. Genevieve Archives, Deed -199 (1772).

33. Bradbury, 260. Native grapes and plums were also used. Captain Pittman reported that a "very enebriating" wine was made from wild grapes "very like the red wine of Provence." Pittman, 98.

34. The wide spacing of houses also prevented the spreading of fires which were so disastrous in Detroit and New Orleans.

35. LT I: Fo. 16.

36. For an example of such a grant, see Langoumois' concession 40' x 60', Feb. 2, 1770. LT I: Fo. 34. Some barns were enclosed with the houses in the village.

37. H. Min., May 18, 1825. Testimony of Pierre Chouteau. The lots in the barn area had all been conceded by 1799. James McKay petition to Delassus Oct. 9, 1799, cited in "McKay et al vs. Dillon," Benjamin C. Howard, *Reports of Cases Argued and Adjudged in the Supreme Court of the United States, January Term, 1846.* (Boston, 1846) 4: 421.

THE COMMONS

IN THE COLONIAL PERIOD of St. Louis the commons *(commune)* was a large body of land used jointly by the inhabitants of the village for the grazing of cattle and the procurement of building timber and firewood.[1] It was a part of the original master plan, like the village proper and the fields reserved for cultivation.[2] As St. Louis grew, so did the commons and its fence was advanced as necessary.[3] The greatest extent of this tract was considerable, for it included the outskirts of the village and all of the Mississippi shore to the River des Peres, a distance of over seven miles.[4]

The commons is an old European institution found in the agricultural

---

1. It was also used for hunting small game. Howard, 4: 441.

2. No specific act of creation is known today. Baptiste Riviere, one of the early settlers, believed that the commons was granted by St. Ange. H. Min., Nov. 23, 1825. Auguste Chouteau in 1806 stated that there never had been a written concession. *ASP,* PL II: 671. Probably it was only a section of the public domain reserved by common understanding.

3. *ASP,* PL II: 671. Testimony of William H. Lecompte. H. Min., Testimony of Pierre Chouteau. Nov. 24, 1825.

4. At its lower end it extended a long way westward and included the village of Carondelet which was founded soon afterwards. H. Min., Nov. 23, 1825. Testimony of Jean Baptiste Lorraine, Sr. Reaffirmed by Baptiste Domine, Alexander Grimaux *dit* Charpentier and Mackay Wherry. So important was their commons to the people of Carondelet, it was stated that ". . . the land which each of the said inhabitants possesses individually, would not be sufficient to furnish them with fuel, and that without said common they would be obliged to desert said village; that the land held individually was purposely chosen for cultivation and without fire-wood" *ASP,* PL II: 672. Testimony of 1808.

communities of many countries. It was introduced from French Canada[5] to Cahokia, Kaskaskia, and Prairie du Rocher[6] and was probably adopted at St. Louis to attract settlers from those places who had been promised the rights and privileges enjoyed under French government. The laws of Spain, theoretically in force in Upper Louisiana, also recognized the commons, or *ejido,* of the farming village.[7]

A great fence bounded the St. Louis commons. This was begun immediately after the founding of the village[8] "at the expense of the inhabitants, who always kept it in repair."[9] The fence itself, referred to as *"la cloture de la commune"*[10] was described by Baptiste Riviere as completed before 1775. It began:

> . . . at the place called Demi Lune, and went back of the Town following the top of the hill down to the Indian Village, where Judge Bent now lives, after that, the common field fence was altered as to take in the Pond, and extended to the *Pain de Sucre,* near the present village of Carondelet and after this time it was so altered as to be connected with the enclosure of the People of the village of Carondelet which extended to the mouth of the River des Peres. The fence was made in various modes, some was made picket fashion, some worm fence, some with trees of their full length and small stakes with riders on top. . . .[11]

The cattle were thus allowed the run of the village streets, the unoccupied space on its fringes and a vast area to the south and southwest.

The maintenance of this great fence year in and year out was a major undertaking and the work had to be carefully apportioned among the

5. In a letter to me dated Dec. 12, 1941, G. Lanctot, Deputy Minister, Public Archives of Canada, wrote: "There were 'commons' in Canada, but they were pasture fields used in common by the people for the grazing of cattle. Numerous ordinances were issued by intendents regulating their use and upkeep."

6. The Kaskaskia and Prairie du Rocher commons were granted to the inhabitants in 1743 *(ASP,* PL II: 182-83) but were probably in existence before that year. The village of Cahokia seems to have used the otherwise unassigned lands of the *"Seigneury of Cahos"* for a commons with the consent of the proprietors and there was no official commons until 1797 under the American Government. Ill. Hist. Colls. 11: 82; and *ASP,* PL I: 20, II: 194.

7. Eyler N. Simpson, *The Ejido: Mexico's Way Out* (Chapel Hill, 1937), 11-13. Such public reservations were also found in New England towns. See "Common Lands," *Dictionary of American History* (New York, 1940).

8. H. Min., July 29, 1825. Testimony of J. B. Riviere.

9. *ASP,* PL II: 671.

10. LT, I: Fo. 1. An early reference is found in the grant to Joseph Calvé, April 31(?), 1766. The Cakokia village fence was so named in 1735. Archives of the Seminary of Quebec. Polygraph 9, No. 42.

11. H. Min., July 29, 1825. The *demilune* was a small stone fortification near the riverbank at the upper end of the village. The *"Pain de Sucre, "* now called the "Sugar Loaf" was a small Indian mound still in existence in South St. Louis at the foot of Wyandotte Street. The worm fence was of a relatively late date, an idea brought to Missouri by the southern Anglo-American.

villagers. A set of regulations for this purpose was drawn up and approved at a public meeting held in the *Chambre du Gouvernement* on September 22, 1782. The procedure to be followed was specified in some detail. The general supervisor was called the *syndic*. Each section of the fence was assigned to an individual who was required to mark it with his entire name and to keep it in repair. Before the grain planting time in the adjoining fields—April 15 was the date set—the fence had to be put in good condition. A set of sixteen arbitrators or umpires (working in two teams to check on each other) was appointed to inspect the work and report defective sections.

The owner of the fence was responsible for any damage done in the grainfields by cattle breaking through. It was expressly forbidden to climb a fence and the act of deliberately making a breach was a serious offense. A schedule of fines was set up from which the public works of the village were to benefit. Imprisonment could be demanded for citizens, and whipping for slaves.[12] The St. Louis commons was nearly eighteen years old when these regulations were formally enacted, but similar usages had evidently been in effect prior to that time. As to their application, Lecompte stated that they "were considered as laws, and enforced as such."[13]

The owners sometimes took turns watching the cattle to keep them from breaking the fences,[14] but for the most part horses, cows, and hogs all ran at large on the commons. John Bradbury, a visiting English botanist, discoursing on the difficulties of hog raising under this system, wrote:

> The hogs live on strawberries, hazel and hickory nuts, acorns and roots, and must be occasionally sought for in the woods, to prevent them from becoming entirely wild. On these occasions, the proprietor fills his saddle bags with the ears of Indian corn, with which he mounts his horse, generally with his rifle on his shoulder. If he finds them within

---

12. Billon, 217-20. Similar fencing regulations for Ste. Genevieve dated 1778 are quoted in Dorrance, 24, 25. Later documents pertaining to the fences of Ste. Genevieve and Florissant may be found in Billon, 258, 259, 273, 274.

At Cahokia the communal fencing program persisted until later years. A set of regulations of 1808 for fencing the commonfields is recorded in the Belleville, Ill., St. Clair County Archives, Book of Deeds B., 421-23. It begins: "The existence of all the individuals at Cahokia demands absolutely that the Commonfields should be well enclosed constantly for its preservation so that each and every person may sow or plant in the said Commonfields." The fence was to be five French feet high and open from November 15 until March 20 annually. The *greffier* (or clerk), who kept the register of lands and fence brands, was paid two minots of wheat by each proprietor for each two-year period.

13. *ASP*, PL II: 671.

14. H. Min., July 30, 1825.

three or four miles of his house, he thinks himself fortunate; but it sometimes happens that he is two days in "hunting them up" as they term it. When he finds them, he throws down an ear of corn, which they devour, and he rides gently towards home, with the whole herd screaming after him. When they are almost inclined to give up the chase, he throws down another ear, which practice he continues until he brings them into the yard, where he shuts them up, and feeds them. Here they remain until the morning, when he again feeds them, marks the young pigs, sets them at liberty, and probably does not see them again for a fortnight or three weeks.[15]

In 1771 or earlier, lands for the new suburb of *Prairie à Catalan* (also called *Vide Poche, Louisbourg, Pain de Sucre,* and *Carondelet*) were officially alienated from the St. Louis commons.[16] Two attempts by private citizens to cultivate land in the area, however, met with spirited opposition and were defeated.[17] The commons reached its greatest size about 1786,[18] and declined as an institution soon afterwards.

By 1796 the great fence had been abandoned altogether and from then on large sections passed into private hands. At the close of the colonial period parts of commons were still used for wood-gathering and pasture.[19] The institution was recognized in *Laws of Missouri Territory* of 1813 with a proviso against unnecessary and wanton cutting of timber,[20] and as late as the 1820s a large part of the town's firewood was coming from the commons seven or eight miles down the river.[21] In the American period the citizens of St. Louis claimed 4,293 *arpents* as still in public ownership[22] and what remained was gradually sold off until today

---

15. Bradbury, 260, 261.

16. The first recorded grants of land were made to Clement Delor de Treget on August 20, 1771, consisting of a village lot 200 feet square and a commonfield lot 6 *arpents* wide and 40 long. The settlement grew rather quickly at first. De Treget was followed by Claude Tinon in the same year, by Jh. Hubert Tabault in 1773 and Pierre Martin Diego Thabault, Joseph Boisvert, J. Bte. Menard, and Louis Menard in 1774. Others joined the settlement in succeeding years, each receiving a grant of a village lot 150 feet square (a quarter block) and a strip of one and one-half by 40 *arpents* in the commonfield. LT III, various entries. About 1783 there were thirty or forty families of farmers there, but the population remained stable from then to 1803. *ASP,* PL II: 672. Auguste Chouteau claimed that Carondelet was founded in 1767 and was so named in 1796. H. Min., Apr. 18, 1825.

17. One of these was by Madame Chouteau about 1790. H. Min., Aug 29, 1825. This lay in *La Petite Prairie.* Mme. Chouteau had received a grant of land there as early as 1767 (LT I: Fo. 13) but had apparently lost her rights because she had not developed the property within the customary limit of a year and a day.

18. Howard, 4: 434. See also *ASP,* PL II: 671.

19. Howard, 4: 441.

20. Henry S. Geyer, Comp., *A Digest of the Laws of Missouri Territory* (St. Louis, 1818), 123.

21. Lewis C. Beck, *A Gazetteer of the State of Illinois and Missouri* (Albany, 1823), 330.

22. ASP, PL II: 671.

Lafayette Park in South St. Louis is all that remains.

The passing of the St. Louis commons is not difficult to explain. It is simply another example of a frugal European village folkway breaking up in the abundance and freedom of the American frontier. The Englishman had also established the institution of the village commons on the Atlantic coast in the seventeenth century, but land was plentiful and restrictions on individual initiative were loosening. As the Indian retreated the white man got his land and each frontiersman could stake out his claim in the wilderness without waiting for an advance plan or even a surveyor. By the time these people reached the old French settlements on the Mississippi, all semblance of controlled agricultural land use had been lost in the general scramble for free and cheap farms and town sites.

At the end of the Revolutionary War these Anglo-Americans crossed the Mississippi in a great flood. The Spanish government was helpless to stem the tide and the back country rapidly filled up with farms.[23] During this process the villagers of St. Louis could compare their own inconvenience in maintaining the great commons fence and searching miles for their animals with the self-sufficient life of their new neighbors who lived on compact farms and fenced and cultivated when and as they pleased.[24] The result was inevitable; the colonial land system gave way to the Missouri countryside as we know it today.

---

23. Restrictions obviously aimed at the Anglo-Americans were promulgated by the governor at New Orleans in 1797. "In the Illinois, none shall be admitted but Catholics of the classes of farmers and artisans. They must also possess some property, and must not have served in any public character, in the country from whence they came." "Spanish Regulations for the Allotment of Lands" Geyer, 439. Nevertheless by 1804 three-fifths of the population of Upper Louisiana was Anglo-American. Stoddard, 225.

24. An illuminating example appears in the records. One Louis Robert in 1779 objected to "the bad situation of the Commons" at St. Louis and applied for a grant on River des Peres four miles west of the village "to raise different kinds of stock and at the same time cultivate the earth and build buildings there." LT III: FO. 22. In other words, Robert wanted an Anglo-American-type farm. In 1789 the records refer to farms at Petit Rocher south of St. Louis, "enclosed in four- or five-acre lots after the English fashion." STLRA, 2/2/330-31.

THE COMMONFIELDS

THE BALANCE OF THE ST. LOUIS ECONOMY depended on the produce of its fields. Areas for growing grain were laid out and placed under cultivation as soon as possible. The results were gratifying; even the Spaniard Piernas was favorably impressed. ". . . its *habitants,*" reported Piernas of the new village, "apply themselves industriously to the cultivation of the fields, which are excellent, of vast extent, and produce much wheat. If they continue with the energy that they have hitherto exhibited, they will soon obtain their increase and will make the settlement one of the most populous, extensive, well managed and respectable of all that have been established."[1]

The layout of these fields was very interesting and showed a close relation to the land use ideas of medieval Europe. Like the plow lands of the other Illinois Country villages they had a peculiar pattern first introduced from French Canada. The custom there had been to divide up the lands along the St. Lawrence River into long narrow strips running from the river's edge back a long distance into the hills. This gave each farmer a length of waterfront for a landing, a stretch of bottomland for cultivation, and some woodland on the hills. It was the most equitable method that could be devised for sharing the land, and was adopted on both the Lower and Upper Mississippi valleys during the French

---

1. Report dated Oct. 31, 1769. Houck, *Sp. Reg.,* I:73. In the beginning flour and other provisions were supplied by Ste. Genevieve. Pittman, 95.

regime.[2]

At St. Louis there was little or no bottomland, but the plateau west of the village was well adapted to farming purposes. While there were occasional sinkholes and ravines, the land was gently rolling and possessed of good soil. Part was wooded and part open in the form of grassy parks. The latter were called *prairies*.[3] Fields were laid out to utilize these grassy areas and were named correspondingly. There were five of them: *St. Louis Prairie, Petite Prairie, Grande Prairie, Cul de Sac,* and *Prairie des Noyes*.[4]

The first laid out were those on *St. Louis Prairie,* immediately west of the village.[5] As in the case of the village lots, grants were made verbally until 1766. The first one recorded in the *Livres Terreins*—to Joseph Calve on April 31, 1766—mentions that an adjoining strip was already under cultivation by one Dubé.[6] It was the policy to grant farmlands in proportion to the number of village lots held[7] and Calvé got a strip of two *arpents* front corresponding to his double lot in the village. This tract had a length of forty *arpents* (about a mile and one-half), which

2. This pattern was used at Detroit as early as 1707. *ASP,* PL I: 282. In Louisiana the strips ran from the river far back into the cypress swamps. In the American Bottom across from St. Louis they ran to the base of the limestone cliffs which form the horizon on the east; this was also done west of the river in the original *Grande Champs* of Ste. Genevieve after about 1750. The width of these strips was measured in "Paris acres" or *arpents* (180 French feet or 192½ English feet) and the length varied with the width of the bottomland. Some of these tracts as little as one *arpent* wide were over two miles long. "Strip farming" was a medieval land pattern found in England, France and Germany. Its establishment In Canada is obscure. James W. Thompson in The *Middle Ages, 300-1500* (New York, 1931) II: 726, discusses the European village farmlands in a general way without reference to any particular country. For an interesting essay and maps on English practice see Chapter VII, "Village Plans and Planning" in George C. Homans, *English Villagers of the Thirteenth Century* (Cambridge, Mass., 1941). This idea was introduced into New England; fields at Wethersfield, Connecticut (1640), and Dorchester, Massachusetts (1660), for instance, were laid out similarly. Chas. O. Paullin, Ed., *Atlas of the Historical Geography of the United States,* plates 41D, 43B).

3. The open or prairie land was thought to have been caused by fires set by the Indians. George Henri Victor Collot, *A Journey in North America* (Paris, 1826; reprint, Firenze, 1924) I: 244, II: 154, 155. Schultz, II: 69, 70. It represented a transition between the Great Plains of the West and the unbroken forest of the East. Baptiste Riviere, who came to St. Louis in 1764, stated that in this area "the grass grew in great abundance everywhere, and of the best quality." H. Min., July 29, 1825.

4. Other nearby grasslands less well known were "Orchard Prairie," "Prairie of the White Ox," and the "Prairie of the Three Bulls." No contemporary account of the dividing up of these lands is known to exist. The area became very valuable as city real estate and through surveys and legal investigations a large amount of historical information was recorded in the nineteenth century.

5. Henry W. Williams, *History, Abstracts of Title, Evidences of Location, &c, Relating to the Common Field Lots of the South Grand Prairie and Cul de Sac.* (St. Louis, 1854), 19. Testimony of Auguste Chouteau, 1825. Often referred to simply as "the prairie behind the village" and sometimes as the *"Champs de St. Louis."*

6. *LT I:*Fo. 1.

7. Bradbury, 259.

became the standard at St. Louis, there being no natural limits at which to stop as in the bottomland fields.[8] The most common width was one arpent (192½ English feet), an old unit of measure also known as the "Paris acre."

These first fields extended from the *Petite Rivière* to *Ruisseau des Pierres* and west from the village fence nearly a mile and one-half. In modern terms this was approximately the area bounded by Market, O'Fallon, Fourth, and Jefferson streets. They were separated from the village by the commons fence; the west end was open. Across these fields a strip thirty-six feet wide was reserved for the *"Chemin du Roi,"* or public road, which led to the *Grande Prairie* and, in later years, to the village of St. Charles on the Missouri River. The part north of this road was sometimes referred to as the *"Prairie de la Grange,"*[9] after the great Indian mound then popularly called *"La Grange de Terre"* (Barn of Earth).[10] The *Grande Prairie* was laid out in 1765 or 1766.[11] It began over two miles northwest northwest of the village and was bounded by the *Marais Castor* ("beaver swamp"), a little pond or stream on the north. These fields were so far from the farmers' houses in town that huts were built on them for shelter.[12] One exceptionally large establishment there was Laclede's country place, sold to Madame Chouteau after his death and later to the trader Barthelemi Tardiveau in 1786. It had a house eighty feet long, cabins for blacks, barns, an orchard, and a garden.[13] The Indian attack of 1780 began on the *habitants* working in these fields. One of them, Jean B. Riviere *dit* Baccane was asleep in the house at Cardinal Spring when he was kidnapped and carried off to Chicago.[14]

---

8. The field length of forty *arpents* was used at Detroit as early as 1747. *ASP,* PL I: 306. An idea of the colonial surveyor's units of measure is found in the instructions from Antonio Soulard to John Evans for surveying lands at Cape Girardeau in 1797: "The measure which is used in this Province is the Paris Acre of 180 feet French of 12 In: French to the foot [?]: This measure subdivides itself in the surveying by Poles each Pole 18 feet. So that 10 Poles make the acre...." A. P. Nasatir, "John Evans, Explorer and Surveyor," *Missouri Historical Review*, 25 (July, 1931): 592.

9. LT I: Fo. 18 (1768).

10. H. Min., July 10, 1825. Testimony of Baptiste Riviere. Sometimes this mound was referred to as *"la butte"* or *"la monticule."*

11. Williams, 19-20. The first recorded grant in the Grand Prairie was a tract of 2 x 40 *arpents* to Francois Bissonet on May 30, 1766. The adjoining strips had already been allotted. LT I: Fo. 1. Joseph Labusciere got a tract there on Aug. 12, 1766, LT I: Fo. 5, which had been abandoned by Pierre Texier. This suggests that the Texier concession had been made in 1765 and forfeited under the customary "year and a day" clause. His tract was one of several first dimensioned as 2 x 80 *arpents*, but which were later shortened to the customary forty *arpents*.

12. Williams, Appendix 7: 7. Gabriel Bequette built a shelter for workers on his own land, Alexis Marie had one at the *Fontaine à Marie,* and Joseph Marin one on the *Prairie des Noyers,* H. Min., II: 134.

13. STLRA, 2/1/188-190, 2/2/287. The property was 6 x 80 *arpents* in area.

14. H. Min., July 9, 1825.

In 1766 *La Petite Prairie* was laid out in fields. It was situated on the road south of St. Louis near the village of Peoria Indians. This gave it a second name of *"Prairie du Village Sauvage."*[15] It was a group of only eight fields.[16] South of the *Grande Prairie,* at the head of the *Petite Rivière* drainage, lay the *Cul de Sac* field, a relatively small one laid out in 1768 or earlier, [17] and beyond it the *Prairie des Noyers* fields, laid out about 1769.[18] These eventually touched the fields of the village of Carondelet and their fences were joined by the mutual consent of the two villages.[19] With the *Grande Prairie* and the *Cul de Sac* area they comprised a great block of land a mile and one-half wide and six miles long.

Because strip cultivation was the accepted type of farming in this region there was no local French term for it. When the Americans came they called the strips "outlots" and collectively they were known as the "commonfields." These strips were granted to the villagers so that many of them had farms in several widely separated places.[20] The season for cultivation at St. Louis officially began on April 15, as noted above, when the cattle were driven out and the fence separating the plow lands from the commons was put in order. Of the management of these fields Christian Schultz wrote:

> The manner of using and improving their respective lots is regulated by law and custom; so that any person who permits his lot to lie idle, or who gets his crops in before his neighbors, cannot derive any profit or advantage from turning in his cattle, as this is only allowed to be done on a certain day appointed, when the gates are thrown open, and the whole prairie becomes a rich and well-foddered common for the cattle of the whole community. This custom is likewise observed at most of the French settlements in this country. They appear to have borrowed it from the Indians, who, in order to save the labour of fencing, always cultivate their maize in one common field.[21]

Because of the shape and proximity of these strips it was necessary to have them formally laid out from the beginning. No official surveyor

---

15. H. Min., June 3, 1823.

16. The first recorded grant was for a tract 4 x 40 *arpents* to "La D. Chouteau" on Aug. 8, 1767, at "the Prairie south of the *Petite Rivière."* LT I: Fo. 13. The adjoining tracts had already been taken up.

17. The first recorded grant was to Giles Henrion, April 30, 1768. The adjoining tracts had already been taken up. LT I: Fo. 17.

18. H. Min., June 3, 1825. Surveyed in 1788 by Pierre Chouteau.

19. Jacob Kissell vs. St. Louis Board of Education in the Supreme Court of the United States, No. 93 (St. Louis, 1855), 57.

20. Whether or not this was done for a rotation of crops in the various fields according to the European custom is not clear in the light of present evidence.

21. Christian Schultz, *Travels on an Inland Voyage* (New York, 1810) II: 55. Schultz was writing at Ste. Genevieve in 1807.

was on hand for this purpose but the process was simple enough to have been done by an amateur. The fact remains that all these fields were in use before 1770, when Martin Duralde was appointed the first Spanish government surveyor in St. Louis. Property lines and corners were marked by stones[22] and blazes on trees. Several furrows between each field were left uncultivated for boundaries and this was called *"endossment."*[23] It appears that there was enough open prairie so that it was unnecessary to clear the woodland—the timber and brushy parts were simply left uncultivated.[24]

Indian corn (maize) and wheat were the principal crops. Tobacco and hemp seemed very promising for a while. Rye, buckwheat, flax, oats, barley, beans, pumpkins, watermelons, muskmelons, and cotton were also commonly grown.[25] A Spanish statistical census of 1791 showed that St. Louis had produced 6,575 bushels of wheat, 8,606 bushels of corn and 4,870 pounds of tobacco.[26] But while the St. Louis area seems to have grown enough food to support itself in ordinary times, serious deficiencies were expected during times of siege when the farmers could not attend to their crops in the outlying commonfields and the village would be jammed with troops and refugees. During the emergency of 1797 August Chouteau, who had contracted for provisioning the garrison, was unable to meet the demand expected and supplies were rushed up from New Madrid. In addition, the Spanish minister in Philadelphia contracted with a Baltimore firm to send by barges on the Ohio River a huge quantity of wheat, rice, corn, salt meat, and whiskey.[27]

The height of the commonfield system at St. Louis seems to have been about 1790, when the fields from the *Prairie des Noyers* to the *Grande Prairie* were enclosed in one fence.[28] But the very size of the layout was its undoing. Vast areas, parts of which were never cultivated, had to be fenced against the animals, and, considered with the commons, the whole setup was inefficient when compared with the Anglo-American type of

---

22. Williams, 17. A limestone surveyor's marker with the Roman letter "M" cut in the top face, said to have been used for Chouteau's Mill Tract (surveyed 1803), is preserved at the Missouri Historical Society.

23. Williams, 159. Testimony of Rene Paul, 1825. See also H. Min., II: 110-11. McDermott, *Glossary,* Thompson, II: 726.

24. Williams, 17. In 1770-72 Duralde found these tracts partly worked and partly *"en frinche."* The cultivated areas shown behind the village on the Auguste Chouteau map appear small and scattered.

25. Stoddard, 227. Bradbury, 260.

26. Houck, *Sp. Reg.,* II: 373-77. The tabulation is here retotalled. It is possible that a few of the inhabitants listed were resident at Ste. Genevieve.

27. Ernest J. Liljegren, "The Commission of Lieutenant Colonel Carlos Howard to Defend the Upper Mississippi Valley Against the English"; typescript (San Diego, 1936), 24, 38-42.

28. H. Min., June 3, 1825. Testimony of Auguste Chouteau.

farm. Governor Zenon Trudeau, after five years in office, wrote a strong report against the system in 1798:

> . . . [St. Louis] has very few farmers and those who follow that call-ing cultivate blindly without the least knowledge except what custom teaches, as is shown by the abuse of enclosing in common the farm lands which are separated one from another by a great distance, in order to prevent the sheep and other domestic animals from entering the cultivated parts. It is true that, in the beginning, necessity may have obliged them to follow that method, which experience ought to make them abandon at this present day, for, since the stockade which they have to make annually is extremely extended, and since the in-terest of all is not the same, in order that the stockade be kept up, the most exact vigilance is not sufficient to restrain the animals and in at-tending in time to its repair. Therefore, the crops are destroyed most years by said animals, and it will continue so in the future if that vicious custom is persisted in. Already the good inhabitants desire to aban-don it, present circumstances also demand that it be done away with in order to further the prosperity of the inland plantations. And their animals abandoned to themselves, as in Natchez, they will begin each one to enclose their farms.[29]

The approval of the government seems to have been all that was needed and the fences were abandoned at once marking the end of the commons-commonfield system at St. Louis.[30]

As exceptions to the general practice there had been a few privately owned farms not in the commonfields. Joseph Labuscière was granted several *arpents* of farmland above the village between the *Ruisseau de Pierres* and the *Ruisseau de la Bellefontaine* as early as 1769,[31] and by 1772 several tracts on *la Prairie Lajoye*[32] were in private possession. Jean Baptiste Lapierre, newly arrived from Canada, was given Cabaret Island in the Mississippi for raising cattle.[33]

Most of the other outlying farmlands were granted when communal farming was breaking up. Several got tracts on the river south of the village. Among these were Silvestre Sarpy, who had an orchard on a tract measuring four by eight *arpents,*[34] and Benito Vasquez, a retired Spanish soldier, who had a hog ranch at Benito's Spring run by a black

29. Houck, *Sp. Reg.,* II: 249.

30. The fences of *Grand Prairie* and *Prairie des Noyers* were abandoned in 1798. H. Min., June 3, Oct. 11, 1825. Williams, Appendix 13. The growing scarcity of fencing materials seems to have been a contributing cause. Stoddard, 220.

31. LT I: Fo. 29.

32. *Ibid.,* I: Fo. 31. The location of the *Prairie la Joye* is shown on the Duffossat Map of 1767.

33. LT III: Fo. 17 (1779)

34. H. Min., Nov. 19, 1825.

man named Pompy.[35]

West of the town, and beyond the farthest commonfields, Louis Robert, Robert Owen, and others were granted lands on the waters of the *Rivière des Peres* in 1779.[36] The largest concession near St. Louis evidently was that given in 1785 to Charles Gratiot, a substantial merchant and trader. Generally referred to as "Gratiot's League Square," it was a splendid tract of land containing about nine square miles and developed with a house, garden, orchard, mill, and distillery.[37] From then on the granting of farms became more general. Most of the land in what is now St. Louis County was taken up by Anglo-Americans before the end of the Spanish period when names like Abbot, Adams, and Allen join the older names like Alvarez, Aubin, and Aubuchon in the annals of St. Louis.

35. H. Min., Aug. 13, 1825. These tracts were fenced individually. Howard, IV: 441.

36. LT III: Fo. 22, 30. Ouin or Owen, an American, was perhaps the first of his nationality to take up lands in Missouri. He claimed a house lot in the Village à Robert as of 1795. *ASP, PL* II: 644.

37. The original papers concerning this grant are kept in what is called the "Land Envelope" at the Missouri Historical Society. The petition calls for 84 *arpents* square, but the Soulard survey and plat of 1796 shows that the tract was 84 x 80 *arpents*. It was separated from the *Prairie des Noyers* fields by a road which is now South Kingshighway.

THE DWELLING HOUSE

FRENCH ST. LOUIS WAS A VILLAGE of dwellings. Except for the church, the cluster of barns on the hill, and the fortifications, nearly all activities were housed in the homes of private citizens or in the small buildings on their lots. There were no retail districts, no waterfront warehouses, and no industrial centers. The private house dominated the scene, and its dependencies were seldom large or numerous. These buildings vanished from the St. Louis riverfront years ago, but an idea of their construction and appearance may be gained from a study of the records.

On the average, each house sheltered about five persons[1]. When large trading parties returned from up the rivers, many houses must have been crowded, for there were no inns or hotels. The size of the individual dwellings varied considerably and probably no two were exactly alike. In the earliest days there were many small and temporary huts, but there were also houses like that of Labuscière which was 66' long.[2] Some tiny cabins were built late in the colonial period. In general, however, the tendency was for house sizes to increase as the village grew and developed.

---

1. Considering an estimated population of 500 persons in 115 houses in 1770 (Billon, 95) and a census of 1039 in 1800 (Houck, *Sp. Reg.,* II: table inserted after 413) and a house count of 180 in 1804 (Stoddard, 219). This may be compared with the 6.3 persons per house in Philadelphia in the period 1753-69. J. Thomas Scharf and Thompson Westcott, *History of Philadelphia,* (Philadelphia, 1884) I: 367.

2. STLRA, 1/1/200-202 (1772).

The prosperity of certain families like the Chouteaus, the Cerrès, and Robidouxs is reflected in the increasing size of their mansions.[3] The first ten sets of St. Louis house dimensions in the records give an idea of size and variation: 15′ x 18′, 24′ x 30′, 18′ x 18′, 20′ x 20′, 16′ x 20′, 18′ x 20′, 15′ x 30′, 20′ x 25′, and 15′ x 16′.[4] A very noticeable feature is the high percentage of houses which were square or nearly square. Nearly all of these houses were of one story, although a few had basements *(caves)* underneath and others attics *(greniers)*. The mansions of Auguste and Pierre Chouteau were raised on high basements in the Louisiana style so that today they would be called two-story houses.[5]

Wall construction, whether of stone or wood, falls into several distinct types which will be discussed later. Log walls looked very much like stone walls from a short distance, since they were usually plastered over. Weatherboarding came later with the Anglo-American from the East.

Two other striking characteristics of the eighteenth century Illinois Country house revealed its architectural ancestry in Canada and Louisiana; these were the steep French hip roof and the porch or *galerie* of

---

3. A crude demonstration of this can be made by comparing twenty consecutive sets of dimensions in the archives for the period 1765-67 showing an average floor area of 4,881 square feet with similar sets for the period 1800-02 showing 6,506 square feet.

4. The old French foot, it must be remembered, was larger than the modern English foot.

5. This shows a change from the Norman farmhouse plan which is usually long and narrow. It is probably due to the abundance in America of long straight timber for rafters, which make a wider house feasible, and the severe winter which favors a compact plan easier to heat.

John F. Darby, who came to St. Louis in 1818, described the two Chouteau mansions as follows:

> Colonel Auguste Chouteau had an elegant domicile fronting on Main Street. His dwelling and houses for his servants occupied the whole square bounded north on Market street, east by Main street, south by what is now known as Walnut street, and on the west by Second street. The whole square was enclosed by a solid stone wall two feet thick and ten feet high, with port holes about every ten feet apart, through which to shoot Indians in case of attack. The walls of Colonel Chouteau's mansion were two and a half feet thick, of solid stone work, two stories high, and surrounded by a large piazza or portico about fourteen feet wide, supported by pillars in front and at the two ends. The house was elegantly furnished, but at that time not one of the rooms was carpeted. In fact no carpets were then used in St. Louis. The floors of the house were made of black walnut, and were polished so finely that they reflected like a mirror. Colonel Chouteau had a train of servants, and every morning after breakfast some of those inmates of his household were down on their knees for hours, with brushes and wax, keeping the floors polished. The splendid abode with its surroundings had indeed the appearance of a castle.

> Major Pierre Chouteau also had an elegant domicile, built after the same manner and of the same materials. He, too, occupied a whole square with his mansion, bounded on the east by Main street, on the south by what is known as Vine street, on the west by Second street, and on the north by what is known as Washington avenue, the whole square being enclosed with high stone walls and having port-holes, in like manner as his brother's.

Walter B. Stevens, *St. Louis the Fourth City,* (Chicago, 1909), 116.

the South. Casement windows swinging on hinges also contrasted with the vertical sliding or "double hung" windows of the Anglo-Americans.

The distinctive *"pavilion"* roof of Normandy, steep at the long sides and the almost vertical at the ends, is found in the older country buildings of the province of Quebec and was brought from there to the Illinois Country.[6] The steepness of the roof was originally dictated by the angle necessary to shed water from thatch, but the form was carried along by tradition after thatch had given way to shingles.

The porch or *galerie* was much in evidence at St. Louis and seems to have been used on one, two, three, or all sides of most houses. This was a Louisiana feature described by Robin:

> . . . the heat of the climate makes porches necessary. All houses have them—some on all sides, others on two sides only, and rarely, on only one side. The porches are formed by a prolongation of the roof with the pitch broken into two planes—just the opposite of our mansards. These roofs are supported by little wood columns with a pleasing effect; ordinarily these porches are given a width of eight to nine feet. The width of the porches offers several advantages, it prevents the sun's rays from striking the walls of the house, thus keeping them cooler; it offers a good place to walk (on the shady side), to eat, sit out in the evening with company and often, in the warm spells of summer, to sleep on. In a large number of houses the two ends of these porches are walled in to make private bedrooms, thus giving two rooms at either end of the house.[7]

He could have added the necessity of keeping rain off the plastered walls and used the description for St. Louis houses. Collot's illustration gives the typical Illinois Country *habitation* an all-around gallery and the St. Louis archives mention these from the earliest years, specifying widths varying from four to nine feet. The ends of these were sometimes enclosed as Robin noted[8] and combined with the lean-to, or *appentit,* found on many houses.

Thatching, common in France and Canada,[9] was used for roofing of the first huts in St. Louis and to a limited extent for barns and other outbuildings throughout the period. But it was a makeshift arrangement at best and a great fire hazard in the dry air of the Middle West. Shingles *(bardeaux)* were cheap in North America where there was plenty of

---

6. Four Ste. Genevieve roofs, supported by heavy hewn Norman trusses, may still be found in the Amoreaux, Ribault, Bolduc, and Guibourd houses. The characteristic pitch seems to have been about 52° on the sides and 72° at the ends.

7. C. C. Robin, *Voyages dons L'Interieur de la Louisiane,* (Paris, 1807) II: 255.

8. Dorrance, 16. Called a *bas-cote.*

9. Thatching is still popular in rural Normandy but in French Canada is now found only on a few barns.

straight-grained wood, and in St. Louis they were the most popular roofing material. Both split and sawn[10] types were used and they were fastened down either with shingle nails *(clous à bardeaux)* or wooden pegs *(à cheville)*. Clapboards *(merrains)* were used for roofing late in the period. These were undoubtedly split boards laid on horizontally like weatherboards. An inventory of the property of the widow Lalande lists various items of a roofer's outfit including a wooden horse for making clapboards, an instrument for boring holes in them, four barrels of wooden pegs, a lot of iron rooftools, and a ladder.[11] Bark of trees was also used on a few barns and other lowly buildings, as it had been by the Indians and by the French in the early days of New Orleans.

Specifications for house building in this period show that most houses had two doors—allowing for one toward the street and one toward the yard in the rear. The type of door generally used is not known. An old photograph of the Lorraine-Lisa house shows that it had double glazed French doors, but it was probably not a typical house.[12] The fact that when the villages across the river were abandoned, the first St. Louis settlers salvaged the doors and windows for the new settlement suggests that they were well made and better than the board-and-batten doors generally used by the Anglo-American in the West. Possibly the St. Louis doors were paneled, for there were joiners on hand to make them.

The average house had four windows. Ordinarily these seem to have been glazed. The French colonies in both Canada and Louisiana had imported window glass from their earliest days, and St. Louis evidently had it available most of the time. By 1798 it was a regular article of trade with Clamorgan, Loisel and Co.,[13] and in 1802 the Cerré estate had a large quantity on hand, both in boxes and set in sash.[14] The French style of casement window, single or double, swinging inward on hinges, was used. They were protected by shutters *(contrevents)* of wood swinging outwards against the walls of the building.[15]

---

10. Billets (or blocks) of wood and froes for splitting them are listed in the archives. The split shingles were probably smoothed with a drawknife. *Bardeaux scie* are referred to as early as 1766. STLRA, 4/3/521. Original examples preserved in the Dubreuil House at Quebec (1719) and the Menard House near Kaskaskia (c. 1800) have their butts neatly beveled.

11. STLRA, 5/2/320-321 (1804).

12. A striking number of early nineteenth-century doors in Ste. Genevieve are glazed, probably representing a carry-over of building tradition from the earlier period.

13. STLRA, 5/2/427-514.

14. Ibid., 6/1/79. How much glass and other building materials were imported from the United States is not yet clear. The first window glass factory in Pittsburgh was opened in 1798. Zadok Cramer, *Navigator,* (Pittsburgh, 1818) 55.

15. Two pair of casements remain in the Jacques Guibourd house in Ste. Genevieve, built in 1806-07. They are twelve light sash with 8″ x 10″ lights. The Ribault house in Ste. Genevieve still exhibits shutters of the old dovetailed *(en queue d'aronde)* type found in France.

Of the interior of these houses we know very little. Only one floor plan has been preserved—a crude sketch of the upper floor of the Auguste Chouteau mansion, which shows it to have had a large central room (probably called the *"la salle"*) and small rooms *"petites chambres"* opening off at the four corners, a floor plan familiar in Louisiana. In the building contracts that have been preserved the average ceiling height is about eight feet. The amount of interior woodwork used for decorative effect is hard to estimate. The joiners in the village could have made fine paneling from local walnut, but a few wooden mantelpieces and one corner cupboard are the only items mentioned in the archives. Ceilings were normally of boards and the walls plastered and whitewashed. The floors were sometimes of the bare earth and sometimes of walnut highly polished.[16] Furniture was listed in quantity and variety in the many inventories which have been preserved.[17]

Iron was not made from Missouri ores during the eighteenth century, but quantities were imported from New Orleans, both in bars for use by blacksmiths and as completed hardware. Spikes *(clous à poteaux),* and nails for special uses like shingling *(à bardeaux),* lathing *(à latter),* and flooring *(à plancher)* were frequently mentioned in the records as were hinges, locks, and hooks. Because of the scarcity of labor in the New World most of the hardware was probably made in France. Such items were sometimes hard to buy at St. Louis,[18] and the markup seems to have been high.[19] Late inventories disclose some large stocks of hardware.[20] The few known examples of early French ironwork used in Missouri exhibit interesting patterns distinctly related to Quebec examples.

Paint is seldom mentioned in the early records and it was probably scarce. While widely used in the thirteen colonies, paint does not seem to have been in the early Canadian tradition. The red lead mentioned in early St. Louis was listed in very small quantities and was likely imported for trading to the Indians as a cosmetic. At the turn of the century three inventories listed paint in several colors. Clamorgan, Loisel and Company in 1798 had:

---

16. Stoddard, 328. "Waxed and as smooth and bright as a mahogany dining table."

17. The furnishings of the St. Louis home of the period would make an interesting documentary study in itself.

18. Houck, *Sp. Reg.,* I: 272. At the end of the period "Iron, steel, nails and castings were boated from the Ohio and its waters." Stoddard: 296. Probably most of this came from the Pittsburgh region.

19. In 1792 Governor Trudeau requested that the government supply him directly from New Orleans with 600 pounds of assorted nails and hardware for four doors and eight windows. He hoped to save 150 *pesos* over St. Louis prices. Houck, *Sp. Reg.,* I: 348.

20. For instance, the inventory of Hyacthine St. Cyr, a builder. STLRA, 5/3/525-555. Inventories include some curiosities like a doorbell (Ibid, 3/2/257-263).

Five barrels ochre weighing 50 lb each
Two barrels green paint weighing 56 lb
Three do white paint weighing 28 lb
⅔ do red paint weighing 18 lb[21]

And Madame Cerrè's estate in 1802 contained:

14 lb ivory black
1½ lb black paint
7 small jugs containing paint
1 barrel red paint
125 lb red color in three barrels
10 lb green paint
6 lb white do.[22]

These are exceptions, however, and the introduction of paint at this late date may be due to Anglo-American influence. The relatively small quantities suggest that they may have been intended for use on interior woodwork or furniture. Varnish is mentioned only once.[23]

Lack of exterior paint did not make the houses drab, however. Christian Schultz wrote in 1807 that St. Louis contained:

> . . . about two hundred houses, which, from the whiteness of a considerable number of them, as they are rough-cast and white-washed, appear to great advantage as you approach the town. . . .[24]

To whitewash *(blanchir)* a building both inside and out was the regular practice among these settlers. Such finish was often mentioned in eighteenth century specifications for house construction and is popularly employed even yet among the French farmers and tiff miners of Washington County, Missouri. Whitewash, known as *eau de chaux* or *lait de chaux,* was made from ordinary plaster and the limestone exposed on the riverbank provided plenty of the raw material.

The great deposits of soft coal near St. Louis were not exploited during the eighteenth century.[25] Houses were heated by open fire, burning driftwood from the river or logs cut on the commons. Chimneys were usually built of stone but sometimes of mud. Although stoves had been used in Quebec[26] and Detroit[27] as early as the middle of the eighteenth

21. Ibid., 5/2/427.

22. Ibid., 5/3/555.

23. Ibid., 5/2/427. Amos Stoddard mentions an excellent Spanish brown paint being manufactured at Cape Girardeau and says that "Many of the inhabitants on the Mississippi paint their buildings with it." Stoddard, 392. Whether or not any of this was sent up to St. Louis is not known.

24. Schultz, I; 109.

25. Joseph Brazeau in 1793 owned a coal deposit on the northern part of the *Grande Prairie,* but there is no evidence of its being mined. STLRA, 1/2/403-04.

26. Peter Kalm, *Travels into North America,* London, 1771, III: 130.

27. R. G. Thwaites, ed., *Jesuit Relations,* (Cleveland, 1896-1901) 70: 57.

century, they seem to have been uncommon in St. Louis. In 1798 Clamorgan, Loisel & Co. were freighting them up from New Orleans,[28] but their cost was probably too high for the average purse.[29]

The method of lighting these houses is not entirely revealed. Candles, candle molds, candlesticks, candle stands, and snuffers are mentioned in the archives, but not in enough quantities, perhaps, to tell the whole story. Probably grease lamps were also used and possibly the simple rush light of rural France. Late in the colonial period lamps appear in inventories, the greatest collection being found in the estate of one Victoria Richelet who had 117 of them, three dozen of which were listed as "glass lamps."[30] The lady evidently ran a shop.

The documents written for real estate transactions often specify the outbuildings which served these houses. For instance, a warranty deed for Nicolas Barsalou's small frame house on a standard-sized lot, included a thatched barn *(grange)*, an old outside kitchen *(cuisine)*, with a built-in oven *(four)*, a hen house *(poullallier)* and a small milk house *(laiterie)*. The whole enclosed by a fence of channeled oak posts, was divided into yard and garden.[31] Louis Perrault's large stone house on a double lot had a building serving as a kitchen, another large building at one gable end of the house divided into a shed *(engard)*, and storehouse *(magasin)*, together with an outdoor oven, latrine, and other useful items. There was also a large garden and orchard *(verger)* of fruit trees, the whole enclosed with a cedar and oak post fence.[32] In such groups there might also be found a granary, stable *(étable)*, slave quarters *(cabanne à négre)*, pigsty *(cochonnière)*, pigeon house *(pigeonnier)*, outside cellar *(caveau)*, or a well *(puits)*. But the house remained the place of business as well as residence and it dominated the village landscape.

Impressions made on American visitors from the East varied considerably. Christian Schultz found "nothing of beauty or taste" in the appearance of St. Louis houses.[33] On the other hand, Yankee Amos Stoddard wrote home that the villagers lived "in a style equal to those in

---

28. STLRA, 5/2/427-514.

29. In 1774 Angelique Desnoyer had a large stove *(poe'le)* with two plates. Ibid., 4/3/534. At public sale in 1805 a "plain stove with two plates broken with its pipe" brought $40 and an old one $10. Ibid., 6/1/79.

30. Ibid., 3/2/501-512 (1796).

31. Ibid., 1/1/54-55 (1770).

32. Ibid., 1/1/202-205 (1775).

33. "I observed two or three BIG houses in the town, which are said to have cost from twenty to sixty thousand dollars, but they have nothing either of beauty or taste in their appearance to recommend them being simply *big,* heavy and unsightly structures. In this country, however, where fashion and taste differ so materially from fashion and taste with us, they are considered as something not only grand, but even elegant." Schultz, II: 40.

the large sea-port towns,''[34] and most opinion seems to agree with the latter. The peaked roof and the shady porches of these French houses were so picturesque and attractive that one wonders why none of the ''Early American'' enthusiasts of modern St. Louis have ever built in the one style really native to the place.[35]

34. Amos Stoddard to Mrs. Samuel Benham, June 16, 1804, in *Glimpses of the Past*, II (1935): 113.

35. The best place to examine early French houses is in Ste. Genevieve, sixty-five miles by highway south of St. Louis. See Charles E. Peterson. ''Early Ste. Genevieve and Its Architecture'' in *Missouri Historical Review*, 35 (January 1941): 207-32. Others may be found in Cahokia, Illinois, and in the vicinity of Old Mines, Missouri.

EARLY MILLS AND FACTORIES

WHILE COLONIAL ST. LOUIS can hardly be thought of as an industrial center, the factories of modern times had their prototypes here in the eighteenth century. Such manufacturing activities as shoemaking, coopering, and gunsmithing were carried on in the dwelling of the artisan. Others, by their nature, required a separate building.

From inventories we know that many households had small handmills for making flour. However, mills run by the power of water, horses, and wind for the grinding of grain and the sawing of lumber appeared early in the Illinois Country,[1] and they were the first industrial plants of St. Louis. On June 20, 1766, Louis Deshetres, Indian interpreter, and Nicholas Hebert *dit* Lecompte, a blacksmith, applied for a lot on which to put a horse mill *(moulin à cheval)* in partnership. This was granted on the condition that it be established within a year and a day, but whether or not it was built does not appear.[2]

Probably the first mill in operation was the water mill on the *Petite Rivière* just south of the village; a large part of the watershed was granted

---

1. D'Artaguiette noted horsemills and a windmill at Kaskaskia in 1723. Mereness, 67. Captain Pittman reported the watermill of an M. Paget at Kaskaskia which ground corn and sawed plank as the first in the region. Pittman, 85. There were three horsemills in Ste. Genevieve in 1767 with one horse apiece. Trenfel, 109. The millstones used in this period were said to have come from a point 250 miles up the Illinois River. Cramer (1818), 129.

2. LT I: Fo. 2.

to Laclède for its establishment on August 11, 1766.[3] Joseph Taillon built the mill itself and on the Dufossat map it is denoted the "MOULAIN À TALION." Laclède paid 400 *livres* cash for it, [4] and, although there was not enough water to turn it the year around, he was able to make a contract with the Spanish government in 1770 to supply visiting Indians with bread.[5] After Laclède's death the property was sold at public auction to Auguste Chouteau, high bidder, along with the machinery for a horse mill.[6] The little sheet of water came to be known as "Chouteau's Pond," and was for many years one of St. Louis's most famous landscapes.[7]

Another early example was the horse mill built by Pierre Lupien for the merchant Antoine Hubert in 1768. Besides its frame building, 35' x 40', Lupien agreed to furnish the machinery, including stones, wheels, ironwork, and everything necessary to put it in working condition, the consideration being 1,200 livres in peltry.[8] In 1771 this mill was leased for a term of ten months for 200 pounds of flour and 300 livres in peltries,[9] and later sold for a 1,000 livres and 4,000 pounds of flour.[10] Although we have no contemporary descriptions of these St. Louis horse mills, the size and shape of the mill houses indicates that they were of the type in which the horse either walked in a circle on the ground or on a circular inclined platform.[11]

Other horse mills are mentioned in the records. Antoine Riviere and Guillaume Bizet built one in partnership (1772).[12] Nicolas Boujeneau operated one in a thatched building 30' square (1775)[13] and Joseph Mandeville one in a stone building 30' x 40' with a stable lean-to for the mill horses (1790).[14] At the close of the century Joseph Taillon, the

---

3. Ibid., I: Fo. 20.

4. Taillon, however, reserved the two millstones and their iron work. STLRA, 1/1/43 45.

5. Houck, *Sp. Reg.,* I: 130.

6. STLRA, 1/1/45-49. Billon, 144. J. Thomas Scharf, *History of Saint Louis City and County,* (Philadelphia, 1883), 158n. 159n.

7. The mill building was replaced several times. The last one was built of stone and stood near Poplar and Eighth streets. The pond was drained in 1853 when the railroad was built into Mill Creek Valley, Scharf: 160.

8. STLRA, 4/2/296-97.

9. Ibid., 4/3/528.

10. Ibid., 2/1/147-148.

11. In the summer of 1817 Obediah Osborn built a horse sawmill in Bonhomme Township, St. Louis County, where "one yoke of common size oxen" or "one span of common size horses" were expected to saw 1,000 feet of plank per day. The animals walked on an inclined "wheel" or "plane." St. Louis Circuit Court File, October Term, 1818, #31, Obediah Osborn vs. James Richardson.

12. STLRA, 5/2/359-384, 2/1/138-39.

13. Ibid., 1/2/371-72.

14. Ibid., 1/1/108-110, 5/3/533-60. It was valued at $350 in the Cerre inventory of 1802.

first miller of St. Louis, had reached the age of eighty-two and was "unable any longer to manage his affairs" but, a miller to the end, he still had a horse mill with two stones valued at $400 among his effects.[15] In 1802, Joseph Robidoux's mill, with eight horses to run it, must have been one of the largest of its kind.[16]

The sawmill *(moulin à scié)* of Captain Jean Baptiste Montigny and Andre Roy, located on the waters of the *Rivière Maline* two leagues above St. Louis, was not a great success. A concession of four *arpents* had been obtained in 1770 and a small thatched house with an earthen chimney built. Although the mill seems to have sawed some boards, the partnership was dissolved two years later. Montigny then leased it for three years to Joachim Roy and François Mandeville for the consideration of 2,000 boards five-fourths of an inch thick and 10' long. At that time there were two saws in working order and equipment for more. Before the end of the month J. B. Bequet had taken Mandeville's place. Later in the year the mill was damaged by a flood and the contract was abandoned, whereupon Joachim Roy agreed for 300 *livres* to take over for twelve months. There were two saws still usable when it was sold to Charles Bizet in 1774, but a few years later the whole property, presumably abandoned, was reunited to the Royal Domain.[17] As late as 1785 planks were procured at Kaskaskia,[18] possibly from the Paget watermill. The number of St. Louis specifications calling for lumber squared *"à la hache"* shows that much of it was being finished by hand in the primitive way.

Two windmills *(moulins à vent)* were to be seen on the St. Louis skyline towards the end of the century. The first was that of Joseph Motard on the hill near Fort San Carlos, the second was built by Antoine Roy near the river. Motard, a native of Avignon, France, referred to in the records as a merchant and goldsmith, probably built it as an investment for someone else to operate. In 1789 Governor Perez granted him a lot 200' square for that purpose, to be developed within three years. A wooden mill was erected but it was evidently not a success. After only fifteen years it was in ruins and sold after Motard's death for only $102. Years later it was remembered as the place where the boys of the

15. On June 30, 1799, Tallon's property was put up for public sale to be divided among his eight children. STLRA, 5/3/514-24.

16. Ibid., 4/3/390-91. Callot (II: 163) remarked that the flour of Upper Louisiana was inferior to that of the Anglo-Americans "owing to the imperfection of the corn mills."

17. LT I: Fo. 31; STLRA, 4/1/187, 4/3/528-30, 2/1/121-22, 5/3/601-04. The Cerre estate in 1802 had "1 set of iron works of a saw mill—170 lb." in the garret. Ibid., 5/3/555-601.

18. H. Min., April 18, 1825.

village played ball.[19]

Roy petitioned Governor Trudeau in 1797 for a tract 600' square north of the village for the same purpose. Military engineers working on the nearby fortifications cleared the project, and Roy built a round stone mill there. Like Motard's it seems to have been a failure for it ran only two years.[20] The structure, however, stood for many years[21] and when St. Louis was incorporated in 1809, "Roy's Tower" was designated as the beginning point for the town limits. There are three good views which show that it resembled the old French tower mills along the St. Lawrence River, a number of which still stand.

One mill of another type, the "floating" mill, was at least planned by Pierre Chouteau who was granted a piece of land for the purpose on October 16, 1799.[22] Although this type is unknown today, Christian Schultz found them common on the Ohio River in 1807. "The mill," wrote Schultz, "is supported by two large canoes, with the wheel between them; this is moored wherever they can find the strongest current closest to the shore, by the force of which alone the mill is put into operation . . . [and] instead of the farmer's going to the mill, the mill comes to him."[23] Whether or not Chouteau's floating mill was ever operated does not appear. By this time there were a number of good water mills not too far away and St. Louis was no longer "short of bread" as it had been in its earliest days.

There were at least two bakeries. In 1775 Francois Barrera was keeping one in a small house on the town lot of Benito Vasquez.[24] He later moved, for at the time of his death in 1803 he was still in business using a bakehouse joined to the rear of a dwelling on the third street,[25] sometimes called *la rue Barrera* after him.

Late in the colonial period Joseph Robidoux built a two-story stone bakehouse on the lot behind his mansion on *La Grande Rue Royale*. He

---

19. Houck, *Sp. Reg.*, II: 159n; LT, IV: Fo. 26; STLRA, 1/1/39-42. Billon, 315. H. Min., I: 169, 171.

20. *Sterling's Abstracts,* Title Insurance Corporation, #2115 St. Louis. Roy's mill stood just above the *demilune* of the village fortifications.

21. The year 1853 is the demolition date noted in an index to Dr. Gustav Baumgarten's sketchbook (Original at Missouri Historical Society) with a pencil sketch of the tower in 1852.

22. Kissel, 73.

23. Schultz, I: 189. A more detailed description of the "floating grist mill" may be found in Cramer (1818), 207. According to Leland D. Baldwin, *The Keelboat Age on Western Waters* (Pittsburgh, 1941), 187, these mills were successful only for light use.

24. STLRA, 4/2/217-223, 1/1/120. J. B. Malveau, sold the property to Joseph Guillot, another baker, in 1780. Ibid., 1/1/121.

25. Ibid., 5/2/309-16. The inventory shows that it contained "two kneading troughs, a large board for dough, five shovels assorted and scrapers, a sieve, a cribble[?] a pair of small scales and various other effects of the trade, valued at five hundred dollars."

seems to have had contracts for making bread and biscuits, probably from the flour made in his eight-horse mill. At Robidoux's death in 1809 his large estate included a complement of baker's equipment listed as: "a large kneeding trough, two small ditto, a wooden jar, two buckets, a water jar, a table, a fire shovel, a rake, two wooden shovels, a pair of small scales, four linen sacks, two leather ditto, five or six bread clothes, three blankets for covering bread, one kettle, two large bread baskets, a lantern, two rollers, a paste knife, a sieve and two pitchers."[26]

The great commerce in skins and furs gave work to a number of tanners at St. Louis. Three are identified in the archives. The first was Paul Sigle, a Maltese, who died in 1769. We know nothing of his shop and equipment except for a large grindstone he ordered from Roussel the mason.[27] Another tanner, Jean Valdy (or Valby) who was in St. Louis for many years had a tannery which he mortgaged "with all the implements, leather of all kinds, tools and generally everything that belong to and is found existing and appertaining to the said tannery" for one thousand *livres*.[28] Jean Baptiste Lorraine, a Canadian furrier and tanner, was in St. Louis as early as 1780. In 1799 Manuel Lisa, an ambitious fur trader recently arrived from New Orleans, bought his house and tannery which was located on *La Rue de l'Eglise*.[29]

Some of the earthenware vessels listed in St. Louis inventories were probably made locally, for there is a record of one pottery late in the period—that of Joseph Eberlein, *"artiste,"* who appeared about 1795.[30] In 1796 he had a house and lot on *Le Rue de l'Eglise* with "various small buildings, in one of which is a furnace for baking earthenware," which he sold to Louis Boissy for 2,000 *livres*.[31] Boissy being out of work, and times being hard, was unable to make payment on the property, which was then sold at a public sale the following year to François Drouin for $285.[32] Drouin, or Derouen, was a young "traveling merchant" from Montreal;[33] whether or not he operated the pottery does not appear. It would be interesting to know more about Eberlein, who was possibly the first artist to live in St. Louis. His name suggests that he was one

---

26. Ibid., 6/79-124. The reason for building a bakehouse two stories high does not appear.

27. Billon, 80, STLRA, 4/2/297-98.

28. Valdy was released from this mortgage in 1782. He appears in the records as early as 1774 and as late as 1792. STLRA, 4/2/348-49, 4/3/405-06.

29. Houck, *Sp. Reg.,* I: 187. STLRA, 2/3/473. H. Min., May 24, 1825.

30. STLRA, 2/3/427, 4/1/81-82. Juan Gilver, a potter, native of France, age forty-eight, is listed in the St. Louis militia in 1780. Houck, *Sp. Reg.,* I: 187.

31. STLRA, 2/3/433.

32. Ibid., 2/3/427-30.

33. Ibid., 1/1/333-34.

of the Pennsylvania Germans who had lately begun to arrive in the Illinois Country.

Other important factors in the St. Louis economy were the salt works on the Meramec River as early as 1768,[34] the maple sugar works *(sucreries)* in the outlying forests and, more distantly, the lead mines in the Ozarks, which had been worked since the early eighteenth century.[35]

---

34. Ibid., 4/2/292. When Pourre acquired this property is not known. There are other salt works mentioned in the records.

35. Pierre François X. de Charlevoix, *Letters to the Dutchess of Lesdiguieres,* London, 1763, 291.

BUILDING CONSTRUCTION

ST. LOUIS BUILDINGS WERE CLASSIFIED from the earliest times by the type of wall construction used.[1] The typical French house was (1) of stone masonry, (2) of palisades, or (3) of frame. Houses of horizontal logs were generally built later by Anglo-Americans. Relatively few of them were to be found in the village.

STONE MASONRY

Stone was readily available at St. Louis from the limestone cliffs at the river's edge and was used throughout the colonial period, both to build entire houses and for the foundations and chimneys of others. The first permanent building—Laclede's headquarters—was of masonry, and there was an average of one stone building erected a year during the next forty years. In 1804 stone houses comprised about one quarter of those in the village.[2]

Stone masonry had the desirable qualities of resistance to fire and rot, and it was firmly in the Canadian building tradition. As early as 1720 most of the houses of Quebec were built of stone[3] and its use began in the Illinois Country at that time.[4] There were several examples among

---

1. The antiquarian Frederic L. Billon, in his lists of early St. Louis houses published in Scharf, 145 *et seq*, was probably the first historical writer to recognize this. Billon arrived in St. Louis in 1818 and knew many of the French buildings and their builders. This firsthand knowledge, supplemented by a tremendous amount of documentary research, established him permanently as an authority on the history of early St. Louis.

2. Scharf, 149.

3. Charlevoix, *Letters,* 20.

4. The house of the lead mining superintendent, the Sieur Renaud, at St. Phillippe seems to have been the first.

the houses of Kaskaskia, and the neighboring Fort de Chartres, built in the 1750s, was the greatest masonry work on the Mississippi River in its time.

Although a number of small barns and outbuildings at St. Louis were built of stone, that material was mostly reserved for the larger mansions. To name some of the most prominent stone houses, Laclede's, mentioned above, was 23' x 60'.[5] The house of Labusciere (built before 1772) was 66' long,[6] the Clamorgan-Chouteau house (about 1785) was 45' x 65',[7] and the Papin-Gratiot house (about 1796) 36' x 52'.[8] These would have been considered large houses in any American village of the time.

Exposed ledge rock being plentiful, the question of its ownership did not come up at first, and prospective builders helped themselves along the riverbank. Toward the end of the colonial period there was a rush to take up title to all unclaimed land and petitions appear for the granting of quarry sites.[7]

A contract for quarrying work was recorded between one Pierre Breuil *dit* Langoumois, "hauler of stone," *(tireur de pierre),* and Pepin the stone mason in 1775. The quality was described as that necessary for a house 20' x 33' with a stone chimney and partition 15' high. The stone was to be quarried and not weathered *(miné et non eventé)* and the work was to be completed in six weeks, with allowances for rainy weather and snow on the ground.[10] Stone was hauled by oxcart from quarry to building site. The drayage in 1799 was five *sous* per load.[11]

The only additional material needed for masonry was lime for mortar and plastering. This was made by simply burning the local limestone over a hot wood fire. The kiln *(fourneau à chaux)* was not difficult to build. The master mason Roussel had one in 1787,[12] J. B. Hubert another in 1795,[13] and Hyacinthe St. Cyr two in 1801.[14] Where the masonry was protected against rain it could be laid up in mud, and many

5. STLRA, 1/1/144-46.

6. Ibid., 1/1/200-02.

7. Ibid., 2/2/318, 319. It was destroyed by fire in 1805, according to a letter found by Prof. McDermott, and succeeded by another.

8. Ibid., 1/1/305-07.

9. For example, Emelian Yosti (Kissell, 70) and J. B. Trudeau (St. Louis Recorder of Deeds, Book C, 79) in 1799 and A. Soulard in 1800 (Kissell, 69).

10. STLRA, 4/3/535, 536.

11. From the quarry of Guillaume Herbert *dit* Leconte. Missouri Historical Society Collections, 4 (1913): 165n.

12. LT IV: Fo. 18. Roussel furnished four barrels of lime for the masonry work in the Sale house of 1770, STLRA, 4/3/526.

13. Ibid., 4/2/227.

14. Ibid., 5/3/525-55.

buildings, including large ones, were so built.

Two contract specifications for stone houses—one early and one late—are quoted here, both to give an idea of the buildings and of the peculiarities of the French and Spanish languages as written locally. The first is from an agreement between Jean Marie Pepin *dit* Lachance, master mason, and Joseph Labrosse, made July 13, 1767, for a consideration of 1,400 *livres* in peltries. It specifies:

(ORIGINAL)

. . . *une maison de pierre de trente pieds de long de dehors en dehors, sur vingt cinq pieds de large aussi de dehors en dehors, avec une cheminée en pierre a chaque pignon de la dite maison—Fournira pareillement toute la pierre et materiaux nécessaire pour la dite maison et maconnerie dont le mortier sera fabriqué en terre; sera fourni aussi par le d. entrepreneur toute la charpente, tout poutre, plancher en madriers de liard, ecary a la hache, a joint carreé, haut et bas, bardeaux, lattes, chevrons, et tout ce qui sera nécessaire, le tout bien conditionné Dans la quelle maison il y aura deux portes d'entre'e et cinq fenetres pour ouvertures, la quelle maison sera elevée pr le plancher d'enbas à un pied de terre, et a huit pieds entre les deus plancher . . .*

(TRANSLATION)

. . . a stone house thirty feet long from outside to outside, and twenty-five feet wide also from outside to outside, with a stone chimney at each gable end of said house; he [the contractor] shall also furnish all the stone and material necessary for said house and masonry, the mortar to be made of earth. The said contractor shall also furnish all the carpenter work, beams, and cottonwood boards squared with the axe and edges butted for the ceiling and floors, shingles, laths, rafters and everything that may be necessary, the whole of good quality. In the said house shall be two doors and five windows. Said house shall be built one foot above the ground, with eight feet from floor to ceiling . . .[15]

The second is an agreement between Santiago Clamorgan, a merchant, and Hipolite Bolon, an Indian interpreter, dated November 13, 1799, for purchase of an eighty-foot lot and construction of a small house, consideration $270. The specification calls for:

(ORIGINAL)

. . . *una casa . . . construida en piedra con merda de tierra, de treinta pies de largo, y veinte de ancho medida por fuera comprehedas las murallas teniendo, quince pies de alto las dhas murallas de una piedra a la otra la cava sera de seis pies de alta, contres aventuras en el cuerpo de la casa aura una muralla de traviesa para separar la en dos y una de estas separaciones sera dividida en dos por una*

---

15. Ibid., 4/3/522-23.

clabazon de madera y una chemenea doble, havra de un planches al otro ocho pies
de alto, y estos plancheos seran enbufetadas tanto el bajo que el alto, havra ig-
ualmente dos puertos, y cinco Bentanas, todos estas aventuras en madera, y la
covertura en texamanis, con clavijas de palo; havra igulamente todo al redor de
la dha casa una galeria de seis pies de ancha, sostenida por potoes en tierra; . . .

(TRANSLATION)

. . . a house . . . built of stone laid in mud, thirty feet long by twenty feet wide, measured on the outside including the walls. The said
walls shall be fifteen feet high, stone above stone and the cellar six feet
high with three openings in the body of the house and a cross-wall to
divide it in two. One of these divisions shall be subdivided by a board
partition. There shall be a double chimney, and eight feet between floor
and ceiling. The boards for the latter shall be tongue and groove. There
shall be also two doors and five windows, all of these openings of wood.
The roof shall be of clapboards fastened with pegs; there shall also be
a gallery around the whole house, six feet wide, supported by posts
in the ground; . . .[16]

PALISADED CONSTRUCTION

Most of the buildings in the Illinois Country villages had palisaded
walls, that is, they were built of posts set upright in the earth. It was
the commonest method in St. Louis, and at the close of the colonial period
more than two-thirds of the houses there were of *poteaux en terre* or *potoes*
en tierra, as written in the French and Spanish records.

The origin of this peculiar type has not been completely traced. Seventeenth century English houses on the Atlantic Coast were sometimes
built that way as were Spanish houses from Texas[17] to California.[18] *Poteaux*
en terre construction seems to have been more or less unknown in France
and Canada, but used in nearly all the first houses in French Detroit,[19]
Biloxi, and New Orleans.[20] Perhaps the first white man's house in what
is now the state of Missouri was the palisaded house of the Sieur de Bourgmond built at the Fort d'Orleans on the Missouri River in 1723. It was,
as he wrote:

---

16. Ibid., 4/2/229-30. The consideration in this case was to have been a draft on the royal treasury.
The house was actually completed by the following October but Bolon, being financially embarrassed, was compelled to default.

17. Stoddard, 195.

18. Rexford Newcomb, *The Old Mission Churches and Historic Houses of California* (Philadelphia,
1925), 79.

19. In 1710 there were only two houses of horizontal logs in Detroit, the rest were palisaded
and thatched. Michigan Historical Collections, 30 (Lansing, 1904): 494.

20. Dumont [de Montingny]: *Memoires Historiques sur la Louisiane* (Paris, 1753) II: 49. That writer
calls palisaded cabins *"cabannes baties de palissades."* Pine logs were used in Biloxi (founded 1710)
and cypress logs in New Orleans.

A house of round posts in the ground *(pieux en terre)* and not framed *(de charpente)*—without ceiling, floor, or chimney—the fire being made in the middle of the floor Indian fashion and a roof of grass supported on rafters just as God grew them in the woods, being neither squared nor finished.[21]

The palisaded type was widely used on the Upper Mississippi and was illustrated by Collot as the "Typical Habitation of the Illinois Country."

St. Louis had a number of small cabins much like de Bourgmond's, especially for temporary shelter in the earliest days while better houses were being built. These were small in size, thatched or covered with bark, furnished with an earthen chimney, and built of round posts called *pieux* or *poteaux ronds.*[22] But this model was generally much improved upon. Posts of cedar and white mulberry—woods which resist rot—made a relatively permanent structure possible, and when these were plastered and whitewashed inside and out, as they usually were, the *poteaux en terre* house could hardly be distinguished from one of frame or even stone. Some of these palisaded buildings were quite large, witness Laclede's country house at *Grande Prairie* which was eighty feet long[23] and one of the Vallé barns at Ste. Genevieve which was 30' x 100'.[24]

A contract between Antoine Hubert and Louis Lambert made July 17, 1769, describes a typical palisaded house of the better class:

(ORIGINAL)

. . . une maison de poteaux en terre de trente pieds de long sur vingt deux de large, avec un apentie a un bout de la dite maison, et une cheminée double en pierres à mantau de bois qui repondra de la maison a lapantie; le tout couvert en bardeau; les maitres poteaux, c'est a dire des coins et dea ouvertures seront de murier avec les proportions qui conviennent ainsi que les cadres des portes et fenetres; dans la ditte maison il y aura quatre fenetres distribuées à placer des lits dans les encoignières, tout le restant des poteaux d'entourages seront en chene blanc bien sain et bien ecury, la ditte maison sera planchée haut et bas, en madriers bien passés a la verlope et enbousetés, avec une cloison dans la quelle il sera placé une porte dans un bout prés la porte de la Sale, la ditte Sale aura seize pieds de long avec deux portes persées vis-a-vis l'une de l'autre et deux fenetres et deux pareils fenetres dans la chambres; lapanti aura une porte et une fenetre, planché

---

21. Paris, Archives Nationales, Colonies, C 13 C, 4:117-25 I.

22. For example, The D'Inglebert cabin. 15' x 18' thatched, without floor or ceiling and with an earthen chimney, sold June 27, 1765. STLRA, 2/1/12, 13. The earthen chimney used in St. Louis was probably similar to that built in Louisiana from the eighteenth century up until the present time. Robin describes it as "made of four wooden uprights slanting inwards with many small cross sticks; the whole plastered heavily with mud." Robin, II; 255-57.

23. STLRA, 2/1/188-190, 2/2/287 (1779).

24. Ibid., 3/2/424-65 (1782).

haut et bas et enbousété. Plus sera pratiqué sous la ditte maison une cave de vingt pieds de long sur quatorze de large at six pieds de profondeur—Sera la ditte maison bien crepié at renduire et blanchie en dédans et en déhors avec du lait dechaut ainsi que l'apantie—et aura la dte maison huit pies entre les deux planchers et aura un pied d'elevation du Res de chaussée au plancher d'enbas et sera le tour de la cave bien contitionné, et tous les bois de la ditte maison ainsi que sa construction sujet a visite par d'expert et gens a ce connaissane; Tous les bois de la dte maison en chene blanc et noyer, tant des portes que des fenetres qui seront bien ferés en tout ce qui sera nécessaire. . . .

(TRANSLATION)

. . . . a house of posts in the ground thirty feet long and twenty-two feet wide, with a lean-to at one end of the said house and a double chimney of stone between the house and the lean-to; the whole to be roofed with shingles. The main posts—that is to say, those at the corners and openings in the wall—shall be of mulberry of suitable dimensions, as shall be the frames of the doors and windows in the said house. There shall be four windows so placed as to allow beds in the corners. The balance of the posts shall be of white oak, well seasoned and squared up. The said house shall be floored and ceiled with boards well planed [?] and grooved, with a partition in which shall be placed one door at the end near the main room. The main room shall be sixteen feet long with two doors cut opposite each other and two windows. There shall be two similar windows in the bedroom. The lean-to shall have one door and one window and shall be floored and ceiled with grooved boards. In addition there shall be excavated under the said house a cellar twenty feet long, fourteen feet wide and six feet deep. The said house shall be well plastered and whitewashed inside and out and the lean-to as well. The said house shall have a ceiling height of eight feet, the floor raised one foot above ground level and the lining of the cellar well made. The lumber for construction shall be subject to examination by experts. All the lumber of the said house shall be of white oak and walnut. The doors and the windows shall be well fitted with the necessary hardware. . . .[25]

Although this specification is unusual for its length and completeness, all of the features mentioned are typical. The average contract simply gives the type of wall construction, the overall size, roof material, and a stipulation as to whether there shall be floors and ceilings. For the rest the workmen were expected to follow established traditions.

The *poteaux* in this type of construction were set in a trench some three feet deep and backfilled. The part buried in the earth was left in the round. Above grade the *poteaux* were left round or hewn about nine in-

---

25. Ibid., 4/3/527, 528.

ches square, depending on the quality of the work,[26] and spiked at the upper end to the plate or mortised into it. Between each was a space about equal to their diameter. This was channelled and filled in with stones and mortar *(pierrotée)*[27] or set with sticks and plastered with mud and grass or straw *(bouzillée).*[28] The former is the Norman and Canadian method,[29] the latter came up from the Louisiana Coast.[30] Outside and inside the wall was plastered, using laths if necessary, making a neat and snug wall.

FRAME CONSTRUCTION

THE FRAME HOUSE WAS NOT COMMON in St. Louis; there were only seven of them after forty years of building—less than three percent of the houses in the village.[31] Such a house was known locally as a *"maison de poteaux sur sole"* or *"sur une solage"* (on a sill).[32] Fitting the *poteaux* into a sill at the bottom (instead of running them down into the ground) required much more carpentry than the popular palisaded house and it also entailed the building of a foundation. The advantage of frame construction lay in separating the structural timbers from the rotting dampness of the earth. For this reason, most of the Mississippi Valley French houses which have survived are of frame construction, even though they were, to start with, the least common type.

The frame houses of Lower Normandy were the ancestors of those in Canada. An early example at Quebec was the Recollet house built in 1620. "The body of this lodging," wrote Father Denis Jamet at the time, "is built of good strong framing and between the heavy timbers is walling 8 or 9 inches thick up to the roof—of good stone."[33] The Kaskaskia manuscripts show that this traditionally French type of construction was being used on the east side of the Mississippi at an early

---

26. Billon, p. 81. The ill-advised statement has often been made that the *poteaux* were driven into the ground. This would have required a heavy pile driver, and the method is very unlikely.

27. An example of 1766 may be found in STLRA, 2/1/10-11.

28. An example of 1768 may be found in Ibid: 2/1/18, 19.

29. Before World War II Rouen, Normandy, was a good place to see this method of filling between posts. It is common in the frame buildings of French Canada.

30. In Louisiana there was no stone, and where a masonry filler was wanted, brick was used (in which case the wall was *briqueté*). In Mobile an oyster-shell cement was prepared. The most common method, however, was to fill in the spaces with a *bouzillage* of mud mixed with Spanish moss, which resisted rot. Robin, II: 255-56.

31. Scharf, 149.

32. The terms *"de belle charpente"* and *"en colombage"* have the same meaning in the Illinois County. *"Potoes sur muralla"* is the local Spanish version.

33. Pierre Georges Roy, *La Ville de Quebec sous le Regime Francais,* (Quebec, 1930) I:75.

date.[34] The Julien Le Roy house on *La Grande Rue Royale* of St. Louis, sold on October 14, 1768, is the first mentioned in the St. Louis archives. It was between twenty and twenty-three feet square, with a stone chimney, floor, and ceiling, and roof covered with shingles.[35] In Missouri the walls of these houses were filled in like the palisaded walls.[36]

Another type of frame construction is described in a contract for a horse mill 35' x 40'. This structure, of white oak and walnut, was to have a stone foundation on top of which was to be built a wall of posts five feet apart, channelled to receive cottonwood boards, evidently like the channelled-post fence described above.[37] This peculiar type of wall was not unique in the village,[38] but there are no surviving examples known.

HORIZONTAL LOGS

The CLASSIC DWELLING of the Anglo-American frontiersman was the cabin of horizontal logs, but it was not well known along the Mississippi River. In 1793 the Baron de Carondelet, governor of Louisiana, reporting on the menace of the American expansion to the security of his own colony wrote:

> This vast and restless population, driving the Indian tribes continually before them and upon us, is endeavoring to gain all the vast continent . . . The wandering spirit, and the ease with which these people procure their support and shelter, form new settlements readily. A carbine and a little cornmeal in a sack is sufficient for an American to range the forests alone for a month. With this carbine he kills wild cattle and deer for food, and protects himself from the savages. Having dampened the cornmeal, it serves in lieu of bread. He erects a house by laying some tree trunks across others in the form of a square; and even a fort impregnable to the savages, by building on a story crosswise above the ground floor. The cold does not fright him, and when a family

---

34. Chester, Illinois. Kaskaskia MSS. Commercial Papers, Vol. I. Contract of Hathurin Charante to build two houses *sur solle* for Sr. Melique, October 1725, the wall posts to be 5" x 7". Contract of Charles Rogue to build the Kaskaskia *présbytère sur solle,* the posts 7" thick. II (Feb. 1, 1731).

35. STLRA, 2/1/34-35.

36. A contract made by the mason Roussel *dit* Sans Souci in 1770, specifies the building of a foundation and the filling in of the frame with stone. Ibid., 4/3/526 (1770).

37. The specification reads *"les poteaux . . . en cannelle, et entoure en madriers de liard."* Contract between Pierre Lupien *dit* Baron and Antonie Hubert, Dec. 14, 1768. A fair degree of finish is implied by the use of windows, doors and lathing. Ibid., 4/2/296, 297.

38. For instance, there was also the Langoumois barn, 20' x 30', thatched, of *"poteau canelle."* Ibid., 2/1/66. At Ste. Genevieve there was mentioned a corncrib *(cabane à Mahis)* of *"poteaux encannelles.* Ste Genevieve Archives, Deeds, #231.

grows tired of one place, it moves to another. . . .[39]

The horizontal log house seems to have been as novel to Carondelet as the Anglo-American character. Such construction was familiar to the French of Canada, who called it the *"maison de pièce sur pièce,"* but for some reason it was seldom used by them in the Illinois Country. Probably their *poteaux en terre* houses were easier to build.

At any rate, comparatively few log houses were put up in St. Louis during the colonial period. Two early exceptions were the house of Joseph Robidoux,[40] who had just come from Montreal where such houses were very common,[41] and a two-story log building ten feet square on Louis Ride's lot, which may have been a tobacco barn.[42] It is not so surprising to later find John Coons, the first American carpenter and joiner in St. Louis, building for himself a horizontal log house on Main Street about 1786 and selling it to another American resident a few years later.[43]

The phrase *"de pièce sur pièce"* was used to describe these three buildings. At St. Louis the term implied hewn logs, which in Canada were either let into upright corner posts and tenoned, or were dovetailed (*"en queue d'aronde"*).[44] Late in the century the *maison en boulins*[45] appears in the St. Louis records. This was the hasty cabin of round logs referred to by Carondelet. It was seldom used in St. Louis, but was commonly found in the outlying villages of Florissant and Nouvelle Bourbon.[46] By this time the forests were disappearing and it was soon easier in St. Louis to build an American frame or brick masonry house than

---

39. Houck, *Sp. Reg.,* II: 12, 13.

40. STLRA, 4/2/314 (1771).

41. In 1704 over three quarters of the houses in Montreal were of horizontal logs, Paris, Archives des Colonies, *Depot des Fortifications des Colonies,* Piece No. 469. *"Memoire Concernant La Ville et Les Environs de Montreal,"* Lavasseur De Nere, Nov. 15, 1704.

42. STLRA, 5/3/622-23, 2/1/201-03.

43. Billon, p. 399. STLRA, 1/2/407-409 (1794).

44. An early example of French horizontal log construction with dovetailed corners was Fort Kaskaskia, burned in October, 1766. Pittman, 85.

45. *Boulin* is a Canadian word meaning "a log for constructing a house or fence." Dorrance, 62. A contract of 1797 calls for a house "in the English fashion, that is to say, *en boulin.* STLRA, 1/2/375. The instructions to J. B. Trudeau in 1794 for building two cabins in the Mandan County specify that they be "built of logs placed one upon another in English fashion." Houck, *Sp. Reg.,* II: 164. The whole subject of the origin of the horizontal log cabin in America is still very obscure. Nothing has been published to carry ahead the Shutleff-Morison study. *The Log Cabin Myth,* (Cambridge, 1939).

46. Lt. Governor Trudeau reported from St. Louis in 1798 that the Anglo-American houses "are already better than those of the Creoles and Canadians, who were settled in villages thirty years ago." Houck, *Sp. Reg.,* II: 256.

one of logs.[47]

Of all the woods used for lumber at St. Louis, mulberry *(nurier)*[48] and cedar *(cédre)*[49] seem to have been the most highly esteemed for their rot-resisting qualities. Walnut *(noyer)* and oak *(chêne)* were also favorites, the former especially for flooring and the latter for framing. Cottonwood *(liard)* was abundant and commonly used for boards and shingles. Pine did not grow near St. Louis and was not used until later.

---

47. Two examples of the *portable* house occur in the archives. In 1779 Louis Dubreuil sold Louis Perrault some real estate including an orchard and a small wood *portatif* cabin used to guard it. STLRA, 2/1/179-80. When Pierre Dorion died at Petite Rocher on the river below St. Louis he left *una casa ambulante,* 12' x 15', with a floor and ceiling, roofed with clapboards. Ibid., 5/1/173-76, 2/2/330, 331.

48. In Latin, *Morus rubra.* At Kaskaskia Father Charlevoix marveled in 1721 that the villagers used this tree for ordinary building purposes. According to D'Artaguitee (1723), mulberry wood could be expected to last thirty years in the ground without rotting. Mereness, 74. In Louisiana today the creoles call this tree the *nurier à chaise* because its toughness affords long life for chairs. Mulberry, like cedar, was popular for fence posts, palisade enclosures and *poteaux en terre* houses.

49. In Latin, *Juniperus virginiana.* So much cedar had been used at St. Louis by 1788 that none could be found on the stump less than a hundred miles up the Missouri River. Houck, *Sp. Reg.,* I: 271.

CRAFTSMEN

THROUGH THE CHAIN OF APPRENTICESHIP the masons and carpenters of St. Louis were linked to the craftsmanship of Canada, Louisiana, and old France.[1] Their architecture appears in a simple but attractive style derived from the old traditions slowly modified by local factors. Its structural evolution can be explained by the abundance of good timber in the virgin forests of the New World, its external character (*galeries* everywhere), by the warmth of Midwest summers, and its

---

1. I made a motor trip through the rural districts of Lower Normandy in 1938 to verify this. The peasants' wooden architecture of this region is closely related to that of Canada and St. Louis. No other part of France observed seems to have much in common. The French rural vernacular has been studied only in recent years and is not very well understood even now. One of the few good general works is A. Demangeon, *La Maison Rurale en France,* (Paris, 1937). I suspect that at St. Louis there was an evolution of style owing to an increase of Louisiana influence over that of Canada, but I have not been able to prove it. After the Revolutionary War, Anglo-American influences grew very strong, eventually superseding the French.

Little of general nature has been written on the French architecture of Lower Louisiana. Samuel Wilson, Jr., "An Architectural History of the Royal Hospital and the Ursuline Convent of New Orleans," *Louisiana Historical Quarterly,* 29 (July 1946), is the best special study that has been published.

The only comprehensive work on French Canadian buildings is Ramsay Traquair, *Old Architecture of Quebec, A Study of the Buildings Erected in New France from the Earliest Explorer to the Middle of the Nineteenth Century* (Toronto, 1947). Professor Traquair devoted many years of study to these buildings and illustrates the volume with a wealth of measured drawings and photographs.

Interesting similarities will be noted between the buildings of French Canada and those of the Illinois Country. Carpenters brought from France put up the earliest structures at Port Royal (1605) and Quebec (1608). The wooden frames of Canadian buildings had heavy close-set upright members, filled in between with stone and mortar like those of Northwest France. Some disastrous fires hastened

simplicity by the shortage of skilled labor and lack of builders' stylebooks.[2] This truly Creole architecture was in use throughout the Illinois Country before the founding of St. Louis and it was brought across the river by the first settlers in 1764.

"Architects"—in the modern sense of the word—were unknown in colonial St. Louis. Possibly the six military engineers who visited the town at one time or another had some small part in the civil architecture of the place.[3] In general, however, the buildings were designed by the men who built them with their own hands.

Since originality of architectural design was neither expected nor desired, the builder was guided only by the practical needs of the owner and the precedent of his own experience. A good example to the point is the specification for Antoine Riviere's stone house put up in 1773. No plans were considered necessary; the masons simply agreed to put a structure "of the same depth front and height as the house of Mr. Côte, a resident of this post, except one foot more above the rafters and a chimney at each gable end."[4] It is doubtful that many working drawings were made. The crude pencil sketch—apparently a floor plan—on the reverse of a contract for François Cottin's house in 1768[5] is the only

---

the building of solid masonry houses. The Quebec stone was difficult to work and cut blocks were used only on the corners and around openings, the rest of the wall was "smothered" in mortar and whitewashed to give a finished appearance.

The two oldest houses existing in Canada date from the end of the seventeenth century. Like those surviving in the Illinois Country, their ceilings are the exposed wooden floors of the level above and their roofs are supported by fine wooden trusses reminiscent of those in Ste. Genevieve, Missouri.

A large part of the Traquair volume is concerned with the carved decoration of churches, of which there seems to be no trace remaining in the Illinois Country.

2. St. Louis inventories list a number of copies of the well-known volumes *La Maison Rustique* in various hands, but this can hardly be called a builder's guide. A remarkable library, property of the late Pierre Charles Peyroux, who had died at Ste. Genevieve, contained (1795):

> 3 volumes—*Architectural drawing*
> 12 small volumes—*Nouveau Tarif du cube des bois*
> 3 small volumes—*Traite de Bois*
> 1 small volume—*Course of Architecture*
> 2 small volumes—*Modern Architecture*
> 1 small volume—*Art of casting iron*
> 2 small volumes—*Traite de Charpente*
> 1 small volume—*Tarif des Bois*
> 1 small volume—*Architecture Pratique*
> 1 small volume—*Nouveau tarif des Bois*

STLRA, 5/2/384-427.

3. The military engineers of St. Louis were duFossat, Varela, Warin, Vanden Bemden, de Finiels, and Soulard. In the eighteenth century many practitioners worked in both "engineering" and "architecture." The two professions had not yet been as completely separated as they are now.

4. STLRA, 4/3/530-31.

5. Ibid., 2/1/23-24. Built by the carpenter Jean Baptiste Ortes.

example known.

While labor was scarce and expensive,[6] the building trades were definitely specialized from the very beginning, an advantage possible in a community of some size. The first persons to settle at St. Louis were "a party of Mechanics of *all trades*."[7] This provided a contrast with the frontier cabin building of the Anglo-Americans in the Mississippi Valley—where the parts were typically made by the owner and raised with the help of the neighbors. St. Louis craftsmen were identified by trade and generally performed their work (1) as speculative builders—putting up houses on their own lots to sell or exchange; (2) as contractors, furnishing all or a part of the materials and labor; (3) as indentured workmen *(engagées)* or slaves.[8] While there were also general merchants who took contracts for buildings, this was probably done as a sideline aimed to move building materials in their stocks or to keep their *engagées* in steady employment.

Much has been lost in the last century and a half, but interesting particulars concerning St. Louis craftsmen and their transactions found in the notarial records provide a general picture of the colonial building trades. Perhaps the most significant fact was that well over half were Canadian-born.[9]

One of striking characteristics of the eighteenth century contracts which have survived is due to the scarcity of hard money in the village. This resulted in the use of peltries for payment and a great deal of involved barter, often including the furnishing of bed, board, unskilled assistance, nails, hardware, lumber, and the loan of tools and equipment. Here the Frenchman's love of bargaining came into full play.

MASONS

AMABLE GUYON IS THE FIRST STONEMASON of whom there is record. He was born at old Fort de Chartres in 1718[10] and may have

---

6. Pittman wrote of the Illinois Country in the late 1760s: "The price of labour in general is very high, as most of the young men rather chuse to hunt and trade amongst the Indians, than apply to agriculture or become handicrafts. At the Illinois a man may be boarded and lodged the year round on condition of his working two months, one month is ploughing the land and sowing the corn, and one month in the harvest. The only trades they have amongst them are carpenters, smiths, masons, taylors, and millwrights." Pitman, 102.

7. H. Min., April 18, 1825. Testimony of Auguste Chouteau.

8. Only one example of apprenticeship was noted in the archives, and no examples of the journeyman working for a daily wage in cash.

9. Considering the militia roll of 1780, Houck, *Sp. Reg.,* I:184-89.

10. Hyde & Conrad, *Encyclopedia of the History of St. Louis* (New York, Louisville and St. Louis, 1899) II: 961. No masons were among the first arrivals in St. Louis as listed in Billon, 17-18,20.

worked on the great masonry fort erected there in the 1750s. He and his family moved to St. Louis from Cahokia in early June 1764 and he probably worked on the stone headquarters of Laclede's company, which was being built at that time. Guyon occupied a small wooden house and then built one of stone valued at 2,500 *livres* on *la Grande Rue Royale.* There he lived until May 26, 1780, when he was killed on the fields behind the town in the British and Indian attack.[11] Charles Routier was perhaps the second mason. About him we know little except that he was born about 1703, was in St. Louis by 1765, also reared a family in a small house on *la Grande Rue Royale,* owned a one-arpent farm, and died in 1777.[12] No references to his construction work appear in the records, which fact may indicate that he was an indentured craftsman brought in from New Orleans or Canada.

Perhaps the best known of the local masons were Jean Marie Pepin (or Papin) *dit* LaChanse, Antoine Roussel (or Rouselle) *dit* Sansouci, and Hyacinthe St. Cyr.

Pepin is the only craftsman whose personality was recorded. Born in Canada about 1740, he was in St. Louis as early as 1767, when he made a contract to build a small stone house for the merchant Joseph Labrosse. Three years later he made an agreement with Jacques Denis, a carpenter, to exchange some masonry work for the woodwork of a house. By 1772 he was known as a master mason and owned a house, lands, two slaves, domestic animals, and other property. He was appointed to a citizens' committee to improve the drainage of the streets (1778) and was listed among the militiamen of St. Louis (1780). He seems, however, to have been a troublemaker—in official eyes, at least. After being run out of Cahokia for disturbing the peace on the American side of the river, he helped organize a *"Sans Coulottes"* society in St. Louis which caused the Spanish authorities much anxiety. Carondelet, governor of Louisiana, in a secret letter ordering his arrest in 1795, called him "a peevish fellow and an enemy of our Government . . . it is more than likely that he is one of the leaders of this society. . . ." Pepin, excluded from the fur trade monopoly imposed by the Spanish at St. Louis, evidently had made some indiscreet remarks at a dinner party. The talk was reported and Pepin found it expedient to leave for Vincennes a few days later—he stayed there for several months. In any case he escaped being sent down

---

11. Primm, 167. Billon, 37, 196, 197. Scharf, 146. STLRA, 4/2/212.

12. Billon, 37. Scharf, 172. STLRA, 1/1/23-24, 2/1/104. In the summer of 1768 there were four masons and stonecutters among the Spanish company at Fort Charles, but it is doubtful that they ever performed any work at St. Louis. They were Michael Trille, a Spaniard; Antoine de Thaguas (or Tagouais); Joseph Seque; and Pierre Perez. Billon, 55, 57. They probably returned to New Orleans with Piernas in 1769.

the river, and in the following year sold a large stone house, evidently built by him, to Charles Gratiot.[13]

Antoine Roussel *dit* Sansouci was born in the parish of Lachine, Canada, about 1740. He appeared in the records of St. Louis as a master mason in 1768, and was married there the following year. He agreed to quarry, dress, and mount a large grindstone for Paul Sigle *dit* Maltais, a tanner, in 1769, contracted for the Salé and Rivière houses in 1770 and 1773, and laid up the stonework of the provincial jail in 1774. He served in the St. Louis militia and frequently acted in the capacity of constable until his death in 1799.[14]

Hyacinthe St. Cyr was born near Quebec about 1746, coming to St. Louis by way of Cahokia in 1780. He was prominent in St. Louis affairs and built several stone houses and a mill. In the 1790s he lost money on a government contract for the town fortifications,[15] and in 1801 he lost a large amount of his property, including lands at St. Louis, Florissant, and Creve Coeur, buildings, slaves, domestic animals, a horsepower mill, and household goods. All were sold to satisfy creditors. Among his assets in the building trades were one incomplete stone house, two lime kilns, one heavy hammer for breaking stones, two forges with bellows, several anvils, iron parts for a sawmill, a wood-turning lathe, and a large quantity of tools and hardware. Later he retired to Florissant, where he died in 1826, the father of fifteen children.[16]

The St. Louis militia rolls of 1780 name four other masons: Bap. Bibaren (Vifvarenne), Franco Cerio, Luis Laflor, and Pedro Ganon (Gagnon) otherwise unknown to us.[17] The archives name five more of the period: Nicholas Bourisse[18] and J. B. Dumoulin, master masons,[19] Amable Flamant,[20] Pierre Laboineur,[21] and Jacinto Amelin.[22]

---

13. Houck, *Sp. Reg.,* I:184, 191n; II: 125-26. STLRA, 4/3/522, 2/1/69, 3/1/219, 220, 1/1/305-07. Billon 141, 433. Lloydine Della Martin, "George Victor Collot in the Mississippi Valley 1796" (M.A. thesis, University of California, Berkeley, 1935), 40, 41, 43. Liljegren, 20-23.

14. STLRA, 1/2/465-67, 4/3/526, 530, 4/2/297-98. Billon, 124, Houck, *Sp. Reg.,* I: 185, Louis Houck, *A History of Missouri,* (Chicago, 1908), I: 320, 321; Scharf, 173.

15. ASP: PL, II: 549. Probably the fortifications of Vanden Bemden.

16. Billon, 456-57. Houck, *Sp. Reg.,* II: 380n. STLRA, 5/3/525-55.

17. Houck, *Sp. Reg.,* I: 184, 185, 188. The last three were born in Canada: their names have been hispanicized.

18. STLRA, 4/3/530-31 (1773).

19. Ibid., 4/3/467 (1798) and 5/3/555 (1802).

20. Ibid., 5/1/169 (1789).

21. Ibid., 5/3/555 (1802).

22. Ibid., 4/3/484 (1803).

CARPENTERS AND JOINERS[23]

THERE WERE AT LEAST THREE carpenters among the thirty men who came with Laclede to found St. Louis. These were Francois Delin, master carpenter, Joseph Mainville *dit* Duchene, and Antoine Valiere Pichet.[24]

Delin (or Delain) was a native of Limours, France. Little is known of his work in St. Louis. He contracted to furnish Laclede with a large quantity of white oak lumber in 1768, and in 1774 did the carpentry and joinery on the provincial jail, for which he was paid 405 *livres*. He died in 1788, leaving a house and an assortment of effects, including some of the tools of his trade.[25] Mainville lived in St. Louis thirty-one years, but his work is obscure. The records show that in 1766 with Jean Baptiste Langevin he made a contract for furnishing lumber to Antoine Hubert for a house 24' x 30'. The bill of materials included eighty posts twelve feet long, other framing pieces, and 4,000 sawn shingles. Two years later he agreed to build a medium-sized wooden house for one Francois Durcy. In 1778 he was appointed to the committee for study of the street drainage. Mainville sold a large stone horse mill in 1790 and died five years later, leaving a modest estate.[26] Pichet's name does not appear in the recorded archives.

Jacques Denis came to St. Louis early and was granted a house lot in 1765. The following year he made three contracts with the merchant Antoine Hubert. First he sold him a *poteaux en terre* house, (in which he agreed to install a floor and ceiling), and soon afterwards a village lot for one hundred *livres* in hard dollars and two pints of rum (to be delivered immediately). Then he agreed to build an addition to Hubert's house for 1,000 *livres* and four *minots* of corn. In July he sold Hubert another lot, together with most of the materials for a house eighteen feet square, agreeing to erect it (assisted by Hubert's laborers) for 1,500 *livres*.[27]

In the spring of 1770 he exchanged lots with, and then contracted to build a house for, the merchant Chauvin. For this Denis was to furnish all the materials except the nails and other ironwork, the owner agreeing to haul the stone and timber.[28] A few months later he and Pepin the mason exchanged woodwork and stonework for houses they were

---

23. In the St. Louis records the differentiation between a carpenter *(charpentier)* and a joiner *(menuisier)* is far from precise.

24. Billon, 18.

25. STLRA, 4/3/523, 5/1/162-63. Billon, 124.

26. Billon, 18, 141. STLRA, 4/3/521, 4/2/297, 1/1/108-09 5/1/238-44.

27. Billon, 38. STLRA, 2/1/10, 11, 2/1/8, 9, 2/1/7, 8

28. STLRA, 2/1/62-63, 4/2/304-05.

then undertaking.[29]

The same year Denis made two contracts of apprenticeship. On April 4 Francis Baribault, a free man aged about nineteen years living in St. Louis, bound himself to Denis for a period of two and one-half years, in which time he was to learn "the trade and mystery of a joiner." Denis agreed to feed, clothe, and maintain the apprentice, and at the end of his term to provide him with a cabin 12' x 15', shingled, with an earthen chimney.[30] In the second deal, he engaged his own service to Hubert as a joiner for the term of one year, during which he agreed to use his own shop *(boutique de menuisier)* without charge except for breakage, and to train an Indian slave named Joseph. For this Denis was to receive 200 *livres* in peltries, ten *livres* of tobacco, a buffalo robe, a blanket, two coarse shirts, and an adz *(hache)* like the one he was then using. Hubert also agreed to pay up some money owed to Madame Beausoleil provided Denis made up any working days lost "by drink or otherwise."[31] In June 1771 Denis sold a lot and an unfinished cabin to Francois Denaux, a blacksmith, with the right for Denis to live in it until All Saints' Day, when completion was anticipated.[32] After this he disappears from the records.

Two joiners early associated in business—Jean Baptiste Ortes and Jean B. Cambas—who were granted a double lot as partners *("menuisiers associez")* in 1767[33] on which they built a frame house together.[34] Ortes, the better known of the two, was born in the province of Bearn, France, and came to St. Louis in 1765.[35] In 1768 he contracted to build a *poteaux en terre* house, 18' x 22', on *la Grande Rue Royale* for Francois Cottin, the royal crier. Ortes was to furnish all the work and materials except 1,000 shingles, part of the posts and planks, hardware for the doors and windows, and the plastering—the whole to be completed in three months.[36]

The year 1771 was a busy one for Ortes. On April 31(!), 1771, the archives show that he contracted to build a house for Joseph Robidoux, a shoemaker recently arrived from Montreal, for 500 *livres* in beaver or deerskins and three pairs of shoes. This house was to have three rooms and to be built of horizontal logs *(en pièce sur pièce)* of cottonwood, ash,

---

29. Ibid., 2/1/69-70.

30. Billon, 73, 74.

31. STLRA, 4/3/522.

32. Ibid., 1/2/379, 380.

33. LT, I: Fo. 12 (July 10, 1767).

34. STLRA, 2/1/82, 83, 2/1/88, 89.

35. Billon, 443. In the archives the town is given as "Luby, province of Beor." STLRA, 1/2/400, 401.

36. Ibid., 2/1/23, 24.

or walnut.[37] Late in the fall he prepared to build a barn, part of which he was to use for his workshop[38] and at the end of the year he contracted to complete the roof on Louis Vige's house for 165 *livres* in skins, with Vige to furnish all materials and two unskilled helpers. This job he completed, but Vige left town without payment, and Ortes had to fall back on a mechanic's lien.[39]

In 1772 Ortes sold his half of the house built in partnership with Cambas, reserving the right to live in it until the following July. In the meantime, he was to keep the roof from leaking, to build in two corner cupboards and improve the barn.[40]

Nothing more appears in the records concerning Ortes' work except that in 1799 he made an inspection of the buildings at Fort San Carlos for the governor.[41] His name is frequently found as a landowner, as a witness to documents, and in other connections such as his purchase at a sale in 1779 of a pair of crimson velvet breeches and two tin flowerpots.[42] His name appears as a member of the local militia in 1780, and in 1782 he married Elizabeth Barada, born in the old French post of Vincennes.[43] Ortes died in 1814, but his widow survived him to reach the remarkable age of 104 years.[44] Of all the local craftsmen, Ortes alone has an example of his work known to remain—it is a fine walnut armoire in the collection of the Missouri Historical Society, a simple, well-made piece, thoroughly French in character.

Not as much is known about Cambas. He was also born in France— about 1736[45]—and appears in the St. Louis records in 1767. In 1776 he was low bidder for the completion of the village church, the project having been suspended at the death of the first contractor.[46] This and the house built in partnership with Ortes are his only works of which we have record. Cambas served in the St. Louis militia and died in 1784 among the Great Osages. His St. Louis estate, inventoried soon afterwards, was found to contain two small houses, an extensive wardrobe, two large dictionaries of *L'Academie Francaise,* and a large set of carpenter's tools appraised as follows:

---

37. Ibid., 4/2/314. See 148, 149.

38. Ibid., 2/1/88, 89, 4/1/178, 179.

39. Ibid., 4/2/315.

40. Ibid., 2/1/88, 89. His housing problem was solved, however, by buying a small frame house early the following year. Ibid., 2/1/97, 98.

41. Houck, *Sp. Reg.,* II: 269-71.

42. STLRA, 4/2/205-10.

43. Ibid., 1/2/400, 401.

44. Billon, 443.

45. Houck, *Sp. Reg.,* I, 186.

46. Scharf, 1650.

	Livres	Sols
Thirty-five carpenter's planes and jack planes..............50		
Two large gimlets, a draw knife and a hammer...........12		
A lot of old chisels of various kinds and sizes...............15		
A large squaring axe..10		
A saw...8		
Two small saws..2	2	
Three small hand saws...10		
A pair of large scales with weights...........................20		
A large grindstone..10		
A small paper with a lot of screws...........................15		
A carpenter's large bench with a vise........................15[47]		

Pierre Lupien *dit* Baron, a joiner, appeared in the archives when he bought a small house in the spring of 1768. He evidently came from the east side of the river, for he was married in Kaskaskia in 1759. Lupien was among those building for Hubert the merchant, and early in the winter of 1768 he contracted for a horse mill to be delivered in complete working order, "turning and grinding," the following May. The building was specified to be of frame 30′ x 40′, using walnut and white oak, on a masonry foundation. Lupien was to furnish all the timber except what was already on hand in Hubert's yard, and the latter agreed to provide the foundation, twenty pounds of nails, two men to assist in hewing the timbers, and one yoke of oxen to haul them. The consideration was 1,200 *livres* in peltries.[48]

In 1771 Lupien is shown to be an officer of the militia and in debt for merchandise, at which time he mortgaged his house, a slave named Therese, and a billiard hall. The following year he made an agreement with Picoté de Belestre, a half-pay marine officer, to erect and equip a billiard hall at Ste. Genevieve for two-thirds of the profits.[49] Lupien's most important work was the building of the parish church which was to serve St. Louis for nearly half a century. At a meeting on Christmas Day 1774 the townsmen formally pledged themselves to erect a new building to replace the temporary structure then in use and all persons fourteen years old or more were to contribute. The contract, awarded to Lupien on April 19, 1775, called for a structure 30′ x 60′ of *poteaux en terre* with a galerie all around and a lean-to in the rear. The main entrance was to be 6′ x 12′, paneled, and the windows—fourteen of them—seven sash lights high and four wide. The whole was to be crowned

---

47. STLRA, 5/1/119-122. The papers of Cambas' estate were filed in 1818 in the St. Louis Probate Court Files as No. 321.
48. Ibid, 2/1/27, 28, 5/2/355-59, 4/2/296, 297.
49. Ibid., 4/2/315, 317, 4/2/296. Billon, 107.

with a belfry *(clocher)* in the form of a St. Andrew's cross. Lupien began this work but it was incomplete at the time of his death the following October.[50] The following tools were appraised with his effects:

	Livres
Three pair of moulding planes	18
Two medium planes	3
Three carpenter's planes	3
Six pieces of wood for moulding	9
Eight turner's irons	15
Two good files and sundry old ones	3
Seven chisels and a medium compass	12
A large pair of compasses and a screw driver	6
Three moulding irons [bits ?]	3
A small press with some pincers	5
Two hammers, one medium the other small with two gimlets	6
Cooper's tools	6
Three axes	18
Two large jack planes	15
Four saws, two large and one small	15
A hand saw, a large and a small saw	30
A wooden square with the lead	1
Four smoothing irons [plane bits ?]	10
A grindstone	3
A tool chest	6
A carpenter's table	10
Four pieces of wood for the feet of an *armoire*	2

Lupien's business records have not been preserved, but they once showed that he had many accounts.[51]

Pierre Tousignan, evidently a carpenter, appears in the archives twice as contracting for houses. He agreed in 1768 for sixty hard dollars to build a house, 14′ x 18′, of round red oak posts for Jean B. Valleau, a surgeon in the Spanish service,[52] and in 1776 he made an agreement with Jean B. Papillon, a trader, to build a house of mulberry *poteaux en terre* 20′ x 25′, with a stone chimney and a whitewashed interior.[53]

Other names appearing less frequently, but known to have been tradesmen in St. Louis, were Francois Marchetaud, master carpenter,

---

50. Billon, 138. The original document is preserved at the Missouri Historical Society in the "Catholic Church" envelope.

51. STLRA, 5/2/355-59. In spite of the detail of the notarial records, they cover only a small fraction of the business transacted in the town.

52. Ibid., 4/3/525. Houck, *Sp. Reg.,* II: 27.

53. STLRA, 4/2/305-06.

(mentioned in 1766-8);[54] Joachim Roy, carpenter (1772-1801); J. B. Dufaux, master carpenter (1774-1802); Nicholas Leconte, carpenter (1779-1804); Antonio Lusere and Pedro Sorret, carpenters (1780); John Coons, master joiner (1786-1811); Baptiste Tison, master joiner (1794-1805); Jean Baptiste Bricault, master carpenter (1795-6); Pierre Bordeaux, carpenter (1795); and Joseph Seguin, carpenter and joiner (1802).[55] Coons was the first builder in St. Louis from the Eastern Seaboard, a forerunner of the migration that was to engulf French St. Louis and completely change the character of its architecture.[56]

BLACKSMITHS

THE RECORDS TELL US LESS about the blacksmiths. Although a great deal of early St. Louis hardware seems to have been European-made and imported through New Orleans, the local blacksmiths undoubtedly furnished a part, especially when the ready-made stocks ran out.

Perhaps the best known of the dozen or so smiths in the record was Jean Baptiste Bequet (or Becquet) who arrived from across the river in 1765. In what seems to have been an unusual undertaking for one of his trade, he contracted to build a house for Picoté de Belestre in 1768. This house was to be 20' x 25', of red and white oak *poteaux en terre,* floored and ceiled, and roofed with shingles. The owner agreed to furnish the roofing nails, the doors and windows and lay up the *bouzillage* and chimney, and Bequet was to furnish all the rest, including the ironwork and hinges which he may have made himself. He lived in St. Louis until his death in 1797.[57]

Less interesting for his work than his misadventures was Jean Baptiste La Pierre, a master blacksmith who came from Canada about 1779. Some ten years later he had fallen into debt and mortgaged some real estate—later discovered to be not his. One night he absconded with his wife to the American side of the river with furniture, beds, and other

54. The years given are the earliest and latest dates these names appear in the St. Louis Recorded Archives.

55. These names are taken from the militia roll of 1780 and from the archives and the list is probably not complete. Three other carpenters, Joseph Marin, François Sespedes, and Man'l Aug'n Aberon were carpenters with the Spanish company at Fort de Chartres in 1768, but it is not known that they did any work in St. Louis.

56. Billon, 399-400. Joseph Verdon should also be mentioned with the joiners. In 1785 he no longer wished to live with his wife, and a separation of personal effects was made. Verdon got "his gun, bed, clothes, two axes and all the implements of turner and cabinet maker, these being indispensably necessary to him . . ." STLRA, 1/2/412-14. Billon, 228-331.

57. Billon, 430. STLRA, 1/2/417, 4/2/296.

goods (also mortgaged), eventually retiring to Peoria.[58]

Another job done by blacksmiths was furnishing and installing the ironwork of the provincial jail built in 1774, for which Guion and Labbé were paid 132 *livres*. This partnership remains unidentified, unless the former was Nicholas Francois Guion, blacksmith and royal armorer, who lived in St. Louis 1769-1784.[59] Others of this trade were Pierre Roy, who was born on the island of St. Pierre, Canada, and was in St. Louis 1773-1799;[60] Pierre Ignace *dit* Valentine, a free black,[61] and Martin Baram, who sold his house, smithy, "his bed, clothes, his gun, *bijoux*, and arms" all in one deal in 1771[62] suggesting another very sudden departure.

---

58. LT, III: Fo. 17. He was granted Cabaret Island, on which he raised cattle. STLRA, 2/2/333-35, 5/1/169, 4/3/458, 2/3/522. Billon, 253-255.

59. Billon, 226. The latter was possibly Jacques Noise *dit* Labbe.

60. STLRA, 1/1/347, 5/1/61-66, 1/1/349-50.

61. Ibid., 3/1/147-49 (1773).

62. Ibid., 2/1/71, 72. In 1769 he entered a two-year partnership with Silvstre Labbadie as a trader. Ibid., 4/3/525, 526.

Blacksmithing at St. Louis seems to have been at low ebb at the end of the colonial period. Captain Stoddard wrote from St. Louis, March 17, 1804: "I have a small quantity of Iron on hand, but only one Smith to work it. This article is usually sold at 50 cents per pound in this place—and I have known nails to sell for 90 cents per pound. Boards are also about six Dollars per hundred feet. Under these circumstances, I beg leave to suggest whether it would not be well to order a quantity of nails of various sizes from Pittsburgh. They are procured at that place as cheap as in any part of the union." *Glimpses of the Past,* II (May-September, 1935): 94, 95.

WORKS OF DEFENSE

AS THE METROPOLIS OF THE UPPER MISSISSIPPI VALLEY and the political and military headquarters of its western part, St. Louis occupied a key position. In the War of the American Revolution it was to help hold backwoods America against a British invasion from Canada. After the war Spain came to regard it as an important bulwark against Anglo-American expansion in the direction of Mexico. But in spite of its strategic military role St. Louis received little aid from the Spanish governor at New Orleans, and that only in dire emergencies. The distance from any strong enemy base remained its best protection.

The hasty fortifications which were thrown up under threat of attack in the period 1780-1797 are of interest as they reflect the hopes and fears of an international frontier. Although they will never be famous in the history of engineering, in terms of pioneer logistics they were a real accomplishment.[1]

The military establishment of St. Louis goes back to the early years when intertribal Indian wars were a constant threat. The first troops to arrive were a remnant of the French garrison of Fort de Chartres who crossed the river with Capt. Louis St. Ange de Bellerive in October 1765. Because of the troubles encountered by the colonial administrators of Spain at New Orleans it was some time before civil and

---

1. The basis of this section is the fine monograph by the late James B. Musick, *St. Louis as a Fortified Town*, (St. Louis, 1941). It in turn was largely based on documents secured by Louis Houck and others from colonial archives. The Vanden Bemden reports on the projects of 1797 are used here for the first time with the kind permission of Dr. A. P. Nasatir.

military authority was firmly reestablished in Louisiana. In the interim, St. Ange was to maintain a provisional government at St. Louis for nearly five years.[2] The lieutenant-governor of Upper Louisiana was always an army officer.

Of St. Louis as an army post we know little. Capt. Philip Pittman reported the garrison as consisting of "a captain-commandant, two lieutenants, a fort-major, one sergeant, and twenty men."[3] St. Ange, the veteran commandant, shared his quarters with the other officers and his storekeeper. Overhead were kept the stores. A guardhouse with five couches and five straw beds was also accommodated under the same roof.[4] As early as the summer of 1766[5] a militia had been organized but the old French regulars were dropping out and by the spring of 1769 "only ten or twelve unfortunate soldiers, unworthy of all confidence" remained. The exposed position of St. Louis caused great anxiety to St. Ange, who recommended the construction of at least a small redoubt. Laclede offered to rent or sell his stone buildings in the heart of the village as temporary fortifications but nothing was done about it.[6] Fortunately war did not come to the new settlement for another decade.

In 1767 a small task force of Spanish troops and workmen came up from the Gulf and in September passed through St. Louis to establish a presidio at the mouth of the Missouri River. This was to consist of two small forts for policing the river against English traders who often trespassed on Spanish territory. The party, under Lt. Francisco Rui, was provided with two engineers (Guy Dufossat[7] and Joseph Varela) and an elaborate staff plans for design and construction. The forts were actually built[8] although they were never garrisoned in strength and in

---

2. Billon, 69.

3. Pittman, 94.

4. Billon, 49. Trenfel, 190.

5. Roscoe Hill, *Descriptive Catalogue of the Documents relating to the History of the United States in the Papeles Procedentes de Cuba deposited in the Archive General de Indias at Seville*, 129. (July 27, 1766.)

6. Trenfel, 190-193.

7. The Chevalier Guy Soniat duFossat (1727-1794) had an interesting career. In 1751 he came to Louisiana from France as a lieutenant in the "Detached Corps of Marines." Dufossat was sent to the Illinois Country in 1759 "being an engineer of ability to construct and repair several forts, among other, Fort Chartres and the Kaskakias." There he remained some two years before returning to New Orleans. In 1767 he entered the Spanish army and ascended the Mississippi as engineer for construction of the fort at the mouth of the Missouri River. Dufossat retired from the army in 1772, settled on a large plantation below New Orleans and twice served as *alcalde* of New Orleans. Charles T. Soniat, Trans. and Ed., *Synopsis of the History of Louisiana*, (New Orleans, 1903), 3, 4.

8. They were the fort "Don Carlos el Senor Principe de Asturias," a palisaded square eighty feet on a side (including bastions) on the right bank of the river and a small blockhouse, "Don Carlos Tercero el Rey," on the left bank. Houck, *Sp. Reg.*, I: 49-52. The structures as actually built were much more modest than those planned at New Orleans.

a dozen years of existence they never served as much more than lookouts. Settlements had been planned near the forts, but that idea was soon abandoned. The troubles at New Orleans caused the withdrawal of the Spanish regulars in the summer of 1769 and command was transferred to the St. Louis militia. The whole expedition had been plagued with quarrels and desertion and altogether it was probably one of the most mismanaged ventures in western history.

In the following year Capt. Pedro Piernas, who had been successful in establishing a new post across the river from Natchez, was appointed lieutenant governor of the Spanish district of Illinois and the capital was permanently fixed at St. Louis. Piernas arrived in May 1770 to relieve St. Ange. His troops, which were detailed from the Stationary Regiment of Louisiana, were quartered in a house rented from Laclede.[9] But as far as fortifications were concerned St. Louis lay for ten more years unprotected by anything more than the private palisades around the town lots and the commons fence. Spain was losing money on the Louisiana colony and the royal pursers were extremely reluctant to authorize public works.

FORT SAN CARLOS

IN THE WAR OF THE AMERICAN REVOLUTION Spain had at first remained neutral, being opposed to the independence of any colonies in America. But to embarrass England she gave undercover aid and encouragement to the revolutionaries. In line with this policy the Spanish Lieutenant Governor de Leyba, commanding at St. Louis, saw to it that George Rogers Clark got the supplies needed to complete his mission across the river. This included the seizure and occupation of Kaskaskia and Cahokia, and later of Vincennes. In the summer of 1779 open war finally broke out between Spain and England, and St. Louis soon had reason to fear an invasion from British Canada. About the following February, Governor Patrick Sinclair at Michilimackinac received orders to prepare an expedition against the Illinois Country. A large party of English traders and Indians, variously estimated at 750 to 1,200, was recruited. Plans were comprehensive and included the capture and sacking of St. Louis and the seizure of the Missouri River fur trade. From there they were to join other forces on the lower Mississippi who would

---

9. Ibid., 67, 68, 130. Trenfel, 238. H. Min., April 18, 1825. Testimony of Auguste Chouteau.

attack and capture New Orleans and Natchez.[10] In April the party rendezvoused at Prairie du Chien and proceeded down the Mississippi hopeful of taking St. Louis by surprise.

But early intelligence of this movement had reached the town and de Leyba had six weeks to prepare for it. Long portages and shallow headwaters on the route down from Canada made it unlikely that heavy artillery would be brought in by the invaders. The problem lay rather in protection against infantry, which might be expected to take advantage of the rising ground just west of the town to shoot bullets and arrows down into the house enclosures.

De Leyba described the measures taken to prevent this in a report to the governor of Louisiana:

> Having foreseen for a long time the embarrassment in which I would find myself in case of an attack by the English and savages, I formed the project to construct four towers or forts of stone at the four corners of this village—one on the north, the second on the south, the third on the east, and the fourth on the west—for the purpose of defending and [for] the security of this post. Consequently I assembled the inhabitants in a meeting that took place at my house [and] . . . invited them to consecrate themselves and their families to this defense by cooperating each one according to his means. They have all devoted themselves to this with joy and good will and after each one had offered according to his means I collected one thousand *piastres.* Of this amount I gave 400 out of my own pocket in order to lighten the burden of these poor people. . . .
>
> I commenced by ordering one of the towers to be erected on the west which would dominate the major part of this village. This tower was almost finished and a beginning made upon the second one located on the north. After having ordered the foundation to be excavated and the first stone placed, I calculated the expense of the first one. I saw, with pain, that all the contributions would at most be sufficient to defray the expenses of only the first tower and that it was impossible to continue the other ones on account of the extreme poverty and misery to which the inhabitants have been reduced. They [the people] made their last efforts to furnish the 600 *piastres* by depriving themselves of the necessities of maintaining themselves and feeding their families.[11]

According to the custom of the times the first stone of the western tower, which they named ''Fort San Carlos,'' was blessed on April 17,

---

10. James Alton James, Ed., George Rogers Clark Papers, In Coll, Ill. State Historical Library, 8 (1912), cxxvii-cxxix.

11. De Leyba to Galvez, June 8, 1780, in Abraham P. Nasatir, ''St. Louis during the British Attack of 1780'' in *New Spain and the Anglo American West, Historical Contributions Presented to Herbert Eugene Bolton,* (Lancaster, Pa., 1932) I: 244.

1780, by Father Bernard, Capuchin missionary and parish priest of St. Louis. The walls were raised with all speed and the platform for mounting artillery was laid. The last cannons from the Missouri River fort were brought down and set up on the tower, although its parapet was not complete. Technically, it was a *cavalier*—an elevated gun platform— intended to command the approaches from the west. A hasty trench *(retranchement)* about a mile long was dug around the town connecting the new tower to the river at both ends.[12] As events subsequently proved, these measures were adequate.

All the inhabitants were summoned and a reinforcement of militia was brought up the river from Ste. Genevieve.

D-day came on May 26, the enemy advancing "like madmen, with an unbelievable boldness and fury, making terrible cries and a terrible firing."[13] At this point the cannon spoke from the new tower, to the surprise and consternation of the attackers who had been led to believe the village open and unprotected.

The trenches were held firmly against the greatly superior force of the British and Indians, who, however, appear to have been little more than a frontier mob. Apparently it was the unexpected artillery and the discipline of de Leyba joined with the determination of men defending their own homes that saved the day. The presence of George Rogers Clark, colonel of the Virginia militia and hero of Vincennes, also contributed to the common defense. Clark had hurried up from his new fort near the mouth of the Ohio River and garrisoned Cahokia on the American side of the Mississippi with 400 men. His strategy was coordinated with that of de Leyba and seems to have included a successful feint in the way of a river crossing.[14]

The attackers were unwilling to storm the defenses, and after failing

---

12. It probably followed the commons fence most of the way to take advantage of an existing barrier.

13. Nasatir, 246.

14. For a discussion of the modern dispute concerning Clark's part in the defense of St. Louis see James, cxxxiv. According to some accounts Clark was offered the joint command but refused. A footnote in *Brief Notices of the Principal Events in the Public Life of Governor Clark* (St. Louis, 1820), says "The event here alluded to is too little known to History and to Fame . . . the inhabitants, despairing of a successful resistance, deputed one of their most respectable citizens, the late Charles Gratiot . . . to solicit the aid of General Clark, then encamped with his men upon the American Bottom . . . He had but 400 men, but they were the riflemen of the West, the daring sons of the forest, to whom danger was sport, hardship was pastime, death was nothing, and glory was every thing.—He led 200 of his valiant band to the ferry opposite the town of St. Louis, and made a demonstration of crossing, while 200 more were sent below to cross under a bend in the river near the place where Judge Bent now lives.—The Indians were disconcerted at the appearance of this unexpected force, and retired, killing 60 of the inhabitants and carrying 30 into captivity." (3n.)

to attract any sorties from behind them, took out their disappointment on the few people who could be found working in the fields, unconscious of the attack on the town. "It is in the *Champs de St. Louis*," wrote de Leyba afterwards, "where was exercised, in less than two hours, the most unheard of barbarity . . . corpses [were] cut into pieces, their entrails *arrachez* [thrown out], their limbs, heads, arms and legs scattered all over the field. What a horrible spectacle. . . ."[15] The enemy finally withdrew, having killed twenty-one (nine of whom were burned alive),[16] wounded seven, and captured seventy-one persons on the campaign.

This abortive invasion, the most exciting event of early St. Louis, caused the year 1780 to be remembered for generations as *"L'Année du Coup."*

CRUZAT'S PALISADE

Rumors of a second invasion from the north continued to agitate the town[17] and François Cruzat, de Leyba's successor, soon had the fortifications augmented. Plans were drawn for enclosing the village with a stockade eighteen feet high and six inches thick, and construction at a rate of over $2,000 per month was under way by December 1780.[18] A *demilune* or "half moon" was built in stone on the bluff overhanging the river at the north end of the town. This was connected by a curtain wall of palisades nine feet high (only half the original planned height) to the tower of San Carlos and thence around the south side of the town to the river. Again, much of it probably followed the line of the commons fence, some of which was already built in stockade form.[19] Bastions were built at the two western angles to cover the curtains. This

---

15. "What was most disconcerting in the attack, was the confusion and the lamentable cries of the women and children who could be heard from the *azile* (government residence) up to the place where the combatants were fighting and it was only due to heroic courage that the arms did not fall from the hands of the fathers of families who signalled themselves with all imaginable valor on this occasion . . ." Nasatir, 246.

16. Inhabitants to Cartabona, July 2, 1780. Nasatir, 254.

17. On August 2, 1780, John Rogers of the Virginia garrison wrote from Cahokia to George Rogers Clark, "We last Night received Intelegence of White and other Savages being on their way to This place again much larger than the former if they come I expect they will meet with a riciption sootable for such Cattle as they are. . . ." Clark Papers, M.S. Vorhies Collection, Missouri Historical Society.

18. A. P. Nasatir, "The Anglo-Spanish Frontier in the Illinois Country during the American Revolution." *Journal Illinois State Historical Society*, 21 (October 1928): 53, 54. The part played by Auguste Chouteau, who said that he had "traced" the plan and who was sent with it to New Orleans, is not clear.

19. H. Min., July 29, 1825.

great stockade, over a mile long and with four principal gates,[20] was completed by the summer of 1781—over a year after the attack, but still two years before the signing of the peace.

Only four years after construction the stockade was in ruins. This could have been no surprise, for it was well understood in those times that such palisaded works were only temporary. American timber was not considered as durable as European[21] and Chaussegros de Lery, the Canadian military engineer, after pointing out how quickly and cheaply such fortifications could be erected, remarked: "In peace time such forts are not built in the colony because they rot quickly and are useless by the time war is declared."[22] Cedar logs were preferred for this purpose but St. Louis had exhausted the nearby supply and it was necessary to go up the Missouri River over 100 miles for them.

Manuel Perez, who succeeded Cruzat as lieutenant governor, recommended in 1788 that the northwest bastion be rebuilt more permanently in stone, and this was done not long afterwards. Although never quite completed, it had walls thirteen to fifteen feet high, with gun embrasures, a guard room and a powder magazine.[23]

---

20. The four gates were mentioned in the minutes of a council of war held at St. Louis on July 9, 1782, (as well as shown on Perez's map of 1788). At that time there were three batteries in existence and five cannon in the tower. The original minutes are in the Bancroft Library, University of California, Berkeley. Courtesy James B. Musick.

21. ". . .even the People here, agree that the Timber of this Country, rotts much sooner than the Timber in Europe does; but indeed there is no Justice done to it here, for it is cut when wanted, and directly put to use, whatever the Season of the Year is." Lord Loudoun to Cumberland, Albany and New York, 1756. Stanley Pargellis, Ed., *Military Affairs in North America, 1748-1765.* (New York & London, 1936), 266.

The French had early remarked about the perishability of wooden structures in the Mississippi Valley—due in good part to the unavailability of paint as a preservative. Deverges, engineer at New Orleans, submitted a complete design for a masonry fort on the lower Ohio in 1745. Wooden structures, he wrote, "absorb in a few years funds which would be sufficient for building solid works of durability and endurance." *Wilson Transcriptions Ministre des Colonies, Louisiana,* Nos. 52, 53.

22. Pierre-Georges Roy, Ed., *Inventaire des Papiers de Lery,* Quebec, 1939, I: 64. The wooden walls of Fort de Chartres in the early days had to be replaced every four years. Little serious study seems to have been given the design of these frontier forts by modern writers. An example of a general essay on the subject is William E. Barry, *The Blockhouse and Stockade Fort* (Kennebunk, Maine, 1915).

23. An estimate for rebuilding the northwest bastion in stone is included in a plan of the town in Houck, *History I:* 312. Although not entirely legible it shows that the total cost was computed at 2,550 *piastres,* and that the walls were to be about 15 feet (2 *toises,* 2 *pieds*) high and three feet thick.

Just after the transfer of the town to the American government, Captains Stoddard, Lewis, and Clark (the latter encamped across the river preparatory to their expedition to the Pacific) made an inspection of the stone bastion. They found that its walls were "about 15 feet high and as they are pretty well cemented with lime, they are likely to prove durable. This fortification is situated nearly at the upper end of the town, and the view between it and the river is not obstructed by any buildings of consequence. . . . The walls are three feet thick at bottom and a little more than two feet at top. They contain two *embrasures* and a number of loop holes for muskets. But this for-

Not long afterwards the Americans—former allies—began to appear more menacing to Spanish interests than the British had. In 1792 the Baron de Carondelet, the new governor of Louisiana, sent Zenon Trudeau up to command at St. Louis. Apprehensive of the settlements advancing west of the Appalachians, he ordered the strengthening of the fortifications. Trudeau was particularly enjoined to be prepared against the use of the artillery, which might easily be brought in on the rivers from the East.

New plans were drawn at St. Louis and reviewed by the Spanish engineer Don Cayetano Payeto at New Orleans. Some confusion arose during the correspondence and the plans were subsequently lost. The general results of Trudeau's construction program, however, are fairly well understood. They consisted of a square stockade about 192 feet on a side with small bastions at the corners and a shallow ditch. This enclosed the earlier San Carlos tower and provided a place "in which the troops, the ammunition, the provisions, and the most valuable possessions of the inhabitants may be gathered for refuge." The project, which was not to exceed 10,000 *pesos* in cost, also included a stone barracks 25' x 50' to quarter the soldiers near their battle stations (as well as to save the rent which was being paid in the village). The garret of this building served as a weapons room or armory. A kitchen 14' x 14', a vaulted stone dungeon 11' x 14', a powder magazine 12' x 14', and a well complete the list of facilities built within the stockade on the hill. The use of private houses and their enclosures was included in the defense plan,[24] and it seems likely that the ten-foot stone walls with loopholes, surrounding the mansions of Auguste and Pierre Chouteau were built at this time.[25]

---

tification cannot be occupied without some labor and expense. You will observe by the sketch that the walls were never fully completed." Stoddard to Dearborn, St. Louis, March 17, 1804, *Glimpses of the Past,* 2 (May-September, 1935): 94.

As built, the bastion stood for many years near what is now the corner of Franklin Avenue and Third Street.

24. Houck, *Sp. Reg.,* I: 343-49, II: 272. On November 24, 1794, Carondelet recommended to las Casas that St. Louis "be encircled by a good stockade, with its *banquette* and corresponding *glacis.* This first should be defended at the two angles which look on the camp of the quadrangle, by two good redoubts faced with stone; and at the center by the small fort now in existence." James Alexander Robinson, ed., *Louisiana Under the Rule of Spain, France and the United States* (Cleveland, 1911) I: 335-37. General Collot did not think much of the fort (which he saw in 1796) although he did not enter it. He described it as: "A paltry redoubt . . . flanked by four bastions, the sides of which were precisely two feet and a half (the space of a single man) and surrounded with a ditch two feet deep and six in breadth, with an enclosure of crannied planks. A garrison of seventeen men. . . ." Collot, I: 248.

25. These were two feet thick, the loopholes ten feet on centers. John F. Darby , *Personal Recollections* (St. Louis, 1880), 11.

After the Revolution in France, that country began to consider the advantages of regaining Louisiana, which its Bourbon monarchy had ceded to Spain. Ambassador Genet's scheme for invading Louisiana with a backwoods army failed, but in 1796 Gen. Victor Collot, a French agent on an intelligence mission, made a somewhat mysterious visit to St. Louis.[26]

He seemed particularly interested in the subject of fortifications and discussed the defense of St. Louis with Lieutenant Governor Trudeau. The idea of raising the waters in the *Petite Rivière* (Mill Creek) to serve as sort of moat especially appealed to him and at the request of Trudeau sketches were prepared by Charles Warin, Collot's young adjutant. This plan was later published in Paris in engraved form. It called for augmenting the existing fortifications with a strong earthworks at the north end of the village, a number of outlying redoubts and firing trenches and a long *abatis* (entanglement) of felled trees across the commonfields from the flooded reaches of the *Petite Rivière* to the Mississippi.[27] These were features never built, but when the plan was later shown to Governor Carondelet, it served to increase his interest in the defenses of St. Louis.

VANDEN BEMDEN'S TOWERS

AFTER COLLOT'S DEPARTURE it was discovered that revolutionary seeds were sprouting in St. Louis and that the subversive society mentioned previously had been formed in defiance of the royal government of Spain. Added to this threat of a pro-French domestic upheaval was the rising apparition of another war with England and invasion from Canada. The regular garrison of St. Louis then numbered only twenty-eight men and Carondelet took prompt steps to encounter these dangers.

---

26. Collot's own account of this trip is amplified by Lloydine Della Martin's study. He stayed eight days as the guest of Lt. Gov. Zenon Trudeau at St. Louis. On this trip he ascended the Illinois River for 210 miles and the Missouri River to the Osage and Fort Carondelet.

27. The Missouri Historical Society has an original wash drawing in color entitled *"PLAN de la ville de ST. LOUIS DES ILLINOIS sur le Missisipi avec les differents projects de la fortifier par George de Bois St. Lys Ancien offr. Francais 1796."* This includes two highly developed designs for detached works. The identity of St. Lys has not been established. The engraving by Tardieu i'aine published in 1826 as "PLAN OF ST. LEWIS With the Project of an intrenched Camp French" (Plate 27 in Collot's *Journey*) seems rather obviously to have been derived from the St. Lys drawing.

Charles Joseph Warin was born in the province of Lorraine, France, and was twenty-six years old when he died in New Orleans on November 3, 1796, while being detained with Collot by the Spanish authorities. Gayoso at Natchez claimed that Warin was equal to the best engineers of Europe. Martin, 100, 101, 120, 191.

He appointed Don Carlos Howard[28] military commandant of Upper Louisiana late in 1796 and sent him with a secret expedition up the Mississippi to reinforce St. Louis and to suppress British activities farther north.

Howard left New Orleans on November 29 and proceeded quickly up the river. On the way he evacuated and destroyed Fort San Fernando de Barancas, on the site of modern Memphis.[29] Personnel, armament, supplies, and even old iron and nails were taken along for use at St. Louis.[30] The expedition reached the latter place on April 27, 1797.[31]

Louis Vanden Bemden (or Vandenbenden), a Flemish engineer then living at New Madrid, was also sent up to St. Louis to assist with the proposed temporary fortifications and he arrived just before Howard.[32] Considered a highly competent man, Vanden Bemden had been professionally trained in France and was a specialist in hydraulics. He had come about 1795 from the ruined French colony at Gallipolis on the Ohio and had made a local reputation by the design and construction of a water-powered mill on the Bayou St. Thomas near New Madrid.[33]

Howard's plan for the defense of St. Louis was mainly based on the use of foot troops in the field. He had at his disposal a detachment of 100 regulars and the provincial militia which was to be concentrated at St. Louis in case of attack. The river was to be patrolled by a miniature navy consisting of a galley, two *galliots,* and a gunboat. Concentrations of friendly Indians at Cape Girardeau and on the Missouri River also entered into the plan.[34] The new commandant did not consider the site of St. Louis well adapted for fortification and he had been directed not to spend more than 5,000 *pesos* from the royal treasury. However, a contribution subscribed to by twenty-five citizens of St. Louis raised the total to 6,400 *pesos.*[35]

Nobody at St. Louis now liked Collot's plans. Vanden Bemden claimed that although they had made a good impression in New Orleans and

---

28. Lt. Col. Carlos (or Charles) Howard was an Irishman about whom not much is known. He had been in the Spanish service for some years, including a tour of duty as Secretary of East Florida. Liljegren, 4.

29. The site was known to the French as *Ecores à Margot,* the Spanish as *Barrancas de Margot,* and the Americans as Chickasaw Bluffs.

30. Liljegren, 16.

31. Ibid., 25.

32. April 12, 1797. Ibid., 24.

33. Ibid., 24 n4. Houck, *History* I: 155. This structure, built on piles, was praised as ingenious in design and sound in construction.

The spelling "Vanden Bemden" is used here as transcribed for the Nasatir collection from documents bearing his signature.

34. Liljegren, 25-27.

35. Ibid., 32.

elsewhere, they were based on inaccurate data and their scale was too costly for the resources available. The arrival of another engineer complicated planning matters further. Yrujo, Spanish minister at Philadelphia, had employed a French officer—Capt. Nicholas de Finiels, who had seen service in the United States Army—at a salary of 100 *pesos* per month, and sent him west. When de Finiels arrived unexpectedly in St. Louis on June 3, 1787, he found construction too far advanced for a change of plans. He was received with no more than cool politeness and Howard, who considered him more of an artilleryman than an engineer, refused at first to eomploy him or even to show him the working drawings. Eventually he was assigned as Vanden Bemden's assistant but the fact that Vanden Bemden was getting twenty *pesos* per month less did not help matters any. As long as the two men remained at St. Louis the salary readjustment could not be made.[36] Vanden Bemden was also assisted in these works by Antoine Soulard, adjutant of the garrison and official surveyor.

Vanden Bemden made a great show of what was wrong at St. Louis. He could find no good in the construction of the earlier period. Fort San Carlos he thought badly designed, as well as incomplete. It was out of repair and its stockade was not expected to last two more years. The stone bastion had a poor foundation and only "thanks to the loopholes it could be taken for a fort and not a corral for cattle." Furthermore, it was commanded by rifle fire from two large Indian mounds to the north and in turn could not itself cover a deep ravine leading towards the town through which an enemy might approach unchallenged. The *demilune* on the riverbank was *hors de service.*

Vanden Bemden made his plans quickly and submitted them to Howard in memorandum form on May 23. In these he first criticized the Collot-Warin plan as "false in all its parts" and pointed out that the proposed scheme to raise the water in the *Petite Rivière* alone would cost more than the funds available. He then laid out three alternative schemes accompanied by plans and profiles. The drawings seem to have been lost, but the estimates, still preserved in the archives of Seville, were transcribed for the Nasatir collection and are summarized here:

Plan One. Surround the town by a great stone wall and dry ditch. This wall, with loopholes for firing,[37] would be over two miles (1,923 *toises*)

---

36. Howard to Carondelet, June 7, 1797, in A. P. Nasatir, "Anglo-Spanish Rivalry in the Iowa Country, 1797-1798," *Iowa Journal of History and Politics,* 28 (July 1930): 369. Liljegren, 29, 30. De Finiels is perhaps best known for his map of the Mississippi River from St. Louis to New Madrid made in 1797-98, the original of which is in the archives of Paris. On leaving St. Louis he went down to New Orleans and was rehired by Governor de Lemos. Liljegren, 34a, n56.

37. *"Mur crenele, un fosse et glacis en dehors."*

long. In the middle of this wall a square fort about 384 feet (60 *toises*) on a side commanding the town and its approaches. On the river side, three covered batteries crossing fire over the whole width of the Mississippi. Estimated cost ''at the lowest St. Louis prices,'' 70,000 *piastres.*

Plan Two. Reduce the line of defenses to nearly a mile and a half (1,383 *toises),* increase the central fort to about 550 feet (86 *toises)* on a side and replace the stone wall by earthworks.[38] On the river side, two redoubts and a battery *à barbette.* Estimate: 10,000 *piastres.*

Plan Three. Repair and improve the existing fortifications as follows: At Fort St. Louis (consisting of de Leyba's fort on the hill—San Carlos tower—dependent buildings, and the surrounding stockade): install new doors, loopholes, and gun platforms, deepen the ditch and build a new palisade on the earthworks.[39] At the stone bastion: raise the walls, close the *embrasures,* build a rampart and a new powder magazine inside, a *cavalier* on top, and surrounded with a ditch 15' deep. An entirely new feature of the third plan were four stone towers described as *corps de guardes*[40] 39' in diameter and 19' high of rough stonework *(moilon.)* The tops were to be decked over[41] and support gun platforms. On the ground floor, loopholes (the garrison would stand on their beds to fire) and a small powder magazine.[42] The towers were estimated at 1,570 *piastres,* 7 *reaux* and the whole plan at 7,000 *piastres.*

---

38. *''Un parapet en terre, un fosse et glacis.''*

39. The estimate calls for 1,300 split stakes to be pegged to a sill fixed on the crest of the berm. This seems to be the kind of palisade described in M. Blond, *Elemens de Fortification,* Paris, 1764), 14n.

40. A *corps de garde* is defined as a guardhouse or guardroom. Cornelis DeWitt Willcox, *A French-English Military Technical Dictionary,* (Washington, 1917).

41. Caulked with oakum *(étoupe)* and tar.

42. It was pointed out that these *corps de garde* could later be surrounded by *redans* (redoubts) or circular parapets and be connected together by a curtain wall.

Because little has previously been known about these round towers a translation of the original estimate is quoted here in full:

No. 4. Detailed estimate of a *corps de garde* in the form of a tower constructed according to the plan and profile, the materials and workmanship estimated at the lowest St. Louis prices.

	Piastres	Reaux
Wall of rough stone *(moilon)* and lime and sand mortar amounting to 41 *toises* 2 feet 1 inch *six lignes cubes*	1095	7
848 running feet of posts and sills hewn to 12″ x 14″ at 1 ½ *reaux* the running foot	159	—
80 planks 2 ¾ ″ x 11″ x 13′0″ at 6 *piastres* per hundred feet	104	—
11 3″-planks to serve as lintels below the loopholes	16	—
18 planks for doors and *coutilles*	18	—
The fixed frame of the door	6	—
For making a double door	5	—
For making the two doors to the powder magazine	5	—
12 days of carpenters' work to assemble the carpentry of the platform and raise it into place	24	—

This colonial engineering document is of unusual interest. It gives many details—that carpenters were getting two *piastres* per day, caulkers 5 *reaux*. Soldiers were paid 2 *reaux* per day for digging and for helping the carpenters and masons. It affords information on the price of posts, squared lumber, and hardware, and gives the price of hauling from the "port" on the river to the fort as 20 *reaux* per trip by *charette*. Certain ironwork and nails were to be supplied by the royal storehouse *(magazin du roy)*. Further plans included a wooden blockhouse to be built at the edge of the *Petite Rivière*. The south edge of the town was to be protected by a wall with loopholes and the various works were to be connected by a "covered way" starting at the old *demilune* and reaching first to the stone bastion, thence to the towers and eventually to the *Petite Rivière* on the south, if funds permitted.[43]

Plan Three was chosen for its cheapness, if nothing else. The old fortifications were repaired, one of the new towers nearly completed and work begun on a "strong house" by the end of July. At this point the Amercians on the Lower Mississippi seemed to have become a greater threat to Spanish interests than the British in Canada. Colonel Howard was called south to face the new emergency, leaving the completion of the work to Lieutenant Governor Trudeau and Vanden Bemden.[44] By May 18, 1798, when the engineers were finally released, the four new stone towers had been more or less completed, two on the hill[45]

---

30 *livres* of nails for flooring and doors at 4 *reaux*	15	—
2 pairs of hinges for the great door	20	—
Iron work for the door	6	—
2 pairs of hinges for the doors of the powder magazine	5	—
50 *livres* of wrought iron at 3 *reaux* per *livre*	18	6
50 *charette* trips to haul all of the framing timbers, planks and finished work	12	4
50 *livres* of oakum at 2 *reaux* per *livre*	12	4
A half barrel of tar, to be furnished from the Royal Storehouse	—	—
12 days work of a caulker at 5 *reaux* per day	9	—
1 *charette* trip to haul the oakum and tar	—	2
These items total fifteen hundred and seventy *piastres* seven *reaux*, errors and omissions excepted.	1570	7

At St. Louis 23 May 1797   *L. Vanden Bemden*
To Sr. Dn. Carlos Howard.

43. Liljegren, 31-33. See also Houck, *Sp. Reg.,* II: 123-139.
44. Liljegren, 33.
45. One about Third and Olive streets, to cover a deep ravine, and the other about Third and Washington where the road to St. Charles left the town through the commonfield fence.

and two,[46] with a cedar log blockhouse,[47] along the *Petite Rivière*. These made a rough semicircle around the town.[48] The presence of Howard's galleys, commanded by Metzinger, made the year 1797 memorable as *"L'année des galéres."*

When the war scare had passed St. Louis defenses again fell into decay.[49] Spain now had urgent interests elsewhere and even had to defend her homeland in Europe. Louisiana passed back to France and even before the latter could take possession, Napoleon bowed to the inevitable and sold the whole colony to the United States. The transfer of command at St. Louis to Capt. Amos Stoddard of the United States Army on March 9 and 10, 1804, marked the end of the colonial period.[50]

---

46. One about Fifth and Gratiot streets and the other about Second and LaSalle Street on the old road to Carondelet.

47. Near Fourth and Chouteau. The second story of this blockhouse was set on diagonally as was the western American practice (according to Carondelet). Houck, *Sp. Reg.,* II: 13. It was planned in 1794 to use this idea at the Osage fort to be built by the Chouteaus. Ibid. II: 109. The first story of the stronghold was to be of stone ten feet high, the second of horizontal logs, "in the mode in which the American build," nine feet high and diagonally placed. An old example of a diagonal second story blockhouse may still be seen on L'Isle Ste. Helene at Montreal.

48. The works to connect these features were never built and General Collot's suggestion of increasing the water area of the pond at Chouteau's mill does not seem to have been seriously considered as a part of this program. Stoddard heard a few years later that it had been "contemplated to enclose the town by a regular chain of works, and the towers were intended to answer the purposes of bastions: But as times grew more auspicious, the design was abandoned, and the works left in an unfinished state." Stoddard, 219.

49. Most of them were found either incomplete or ruinous by 1799. For instance, the large barracks and other buildings only seven years old, were already on the verge of collapse. Houck, *Sp. Reg.,* II: 270-72. The masonry works continued to exist for some years afterwards. San Carlos tower became a jail, the barracks a courthouse, the bastion a garden, and the blockhouse an *abbatoir.* Others were pulled down for their stone and wood. For example, a printer's press was made about 1819 from oak timbers from the old *demilune* on the riverbank then owned by Thomas Brady, deposition of Stephen Patterson. Hill & Keese vs. Thomas Brady, St. Louis Circuit Court File, April Term, 1820, No. 94. In 1819 the magazine in the old masonry bastion was still used for the storage of powder. *St. Louis Enquirer,* Sept. 1, 1819.

Schultz wrote three years after the transfer of command: "This town has been strongly fortified by the Spanish government, having two forts, two block houses, four stone towers, and one half moon. These encircle the whole town on the land side, and are within gun-shot of each other. Some little care is still taken of the forts and barracks occupied by the garrison which is stationed at this place, but the towers and blockhouses are entirely neglected, and, for want of repairs, already tumbling to pieces." Schultz, II: 40.

There was some talk about rehabilitating the fortifications during the War of 1812, but the frontier had already moved beyond St. Louis and it was the new settlements which faced the Indians from behind their stockades.

50. On March 9 Upper Louisiana was yielded to Stoddard as "Agent of the French republic" and on March 10 he "assumed the Country and Government in the name of the United States." Stoddard to Secretary of War, St. Louis, March 10, 1804. *Glimpses of the Past,* II (1935): 92.

A contemporary visitor left us this pleasant closing picture of colonial St. Louis:

> You would almost believe the houses were united and that the roofs upheld and supported one another, so gradually and so beautifully has nature bent her brow for the reception of this village. From the opposite shore it has a majestic appearance which borrows from its elevated site and from a range of Spanish towers that crown the summit of the hill and lend their Gothic rudeness to complete a picture which scarcely has a parallel.[51]

51. Musick, 107. Originally by an unknown writer published in the *Literary Gazette* of Cincinnati in 1807.

EPILOGUE

I AM GRATEFUL for the opportunity of adding to this essay some notes accumulated since the original printing two years ago. No compilation of this kind seems to remain as more than a temporary achievement; the most diligent historical efforts become outdated as new sources of information come to light. Particularly is this true of any attempt to write early St. Louis history at the present time. Before these words appear in print they will probably have become out of date.

Some of the most important pending documentary publication projects will be mentioned here. Among the subjects treated, the history of Cahokia, now two and one-half centuries old, is receiving particular attention in 1949. In many ways that village was the mother of St. Louis and its history a prolongation back to the very beginnings of French civilization on the Mississippi River. Although divided politically, life on the two banks of the Mississippi is hardly separable. A study of the east bank and of its many English, Canadian, and American visitors will probably reveal further descriptions of colonial St. Louis.

Among the very earliest of these which I recently found while studying Cahokia was that of the topographer Thomas Hutchins, who, as an ensign with Captain Gordon and Lieutenant Pittman of the British Army, visited St. Louis at the end of August 1766. Commandant St. Ange had invited them across the river for a visit and they hoped to borrow boats to get up to the mouth of the Illinois River. Although disappointed by not getting the boats "thro a little jealousy," they were civilly treated. Hutchins left a few notes, among them that the elevated site of St. Louis was "the most healthy and pleasant of any known in the Country." The inhabitants already number 800 whites—"some of them very Genteel and well Educated"—and 150 blacks. Of these, 415 whites and forty blacks were rated as "Gun Men." Also noted were 120 houses, "the best in the Country . . . large and Commodious."[1]

A much later description was sent in a letter to Secretary Alexander Hamilton at New York. According to the writer, who was a visitor in the fall of 1791, St. Louis contained:

> about 300 good stonehouses—has a small garison—a strong Castle, and a tolerable wall nearly around the town—the no. of Militia is computed at 500—it is one of the finest inland towns I ever saw, the situation is delightful . . .[2]

As these descriptions are collected from Eastern archives the picture of St. Louis will be much augmented.

A manuscript map which has very recently turned up in the Thomas Hutchins papers at the Pennsylvania Historical Society shows Cahokia village—probably as of 1766 when it was visited by Ensign Hutchins. The typical land unit as shown was a square block (*isle*) divided into four equal lots 150 French feet on a side. The division of the St. Louis townsite into blocks of four equal lots was almost certainly based on the plan of Cahokia, which seems to have been the model regularly used for all the villages on the west bank in the Spanish period. It is another instance of the transfer of the French traditions to the new villages across the river.[3]

THE COMMONFIELDS

A WHOLE VOLUME OF DOCUMENTS for the first year of Louisiana-Missouri Territory has just been published under the veteran editorship of Clarence Edwin Carter. Most of them relate to St. Louis and

---

1. "Remarks on the Country of the Illinois, etc.," Thomas Hutchins Papers, (MS) Pennsylvania Historical Society, I: 57. The MS version does not collate exactly with the printed version.

2. N. Mitchell to Alexander Hamilton, n.p., February 9, 1792, *Mississippi Valley Historical Review*, 8 (December 1921): 264. Mitchell, like many other Anglo-American writers, mistook St. Louis's plastered log walls for masonry.

3. In 1752 the layouts of the villages on the east bank were "very irregular." Macarty and Buchet to Vandreuil, Illinois, 1752. Theodore Calvin Pease and Ernestine Jenison, etc., *Illinois on the Eve of the Seven Years' War, 1747-1755*, (Springfield, 1940), 427. Kaskaskia in the 1760s was still an irregular town, apparently without standard lot and block sizes. The blocks of New Orleans were divided into smaller, narrower lots. The precedent therefore pretty well narrows down to Cahokia.

neighboring settlements. Many are concerned with the great battle for land titles just after the American taking of Upper Louisiana, and incidentally give an insight into colonial land use practices.

In a memorial signed by some of the leading citizens of St. Louis early in 1806, the commonfields of the town are called *"terres de champs,* or out lots for cultivation,'' thus revealing the local French term for this important institution. It does not seem to have been set down elsewhere. In these papers the compactness of the villages of the Illinois Country is also clearly explained by reference to the prevailing Indian menace.

> . . .hence the necessity of the settlers gathering each night under the forts and within a narrow compass so as to ensure mutual deffense; hence the Custom of Cultivating their lands near each other and in the same Enclosure for the same motives of reciprocal protection.[4]

As to the size of the original grants, the Spanish land policy is recited in the statements of various officials. Each settler could be granted 100 *arpents* of land for himself, 100 for his wife, fifty for each of his children, and twenty for each slave, the whole not to exceed 800 *arpents.*[5] Title to these fields could be completed only by the raising of three crops on that land.[6]

Although evidences of the ancient use of "strip farm" layouts in England, Germany, and elsewhere in Europe are not hard to find, precedent in France has proved difficult to locate. Two works on French land patterns of the Middle Ages were finally brought to my attention by Professor Marcel Giraud of the College de France. These are Marc L. B. Bloch, *Les Caractères Originaux de l'Histoire Rural Francaise*[7] and Roger Dion, *Essai sur la Formation du Paysage Rural Francais.*[8] Block reproduces old maps showing strip farms in France something like those of the Illinois Country. One of these (Plate VI) *"Champs ouverts et allongés dans un défrichment mediéval, ''* shows such a pattern dating back to the seventh century A.D.

As stated earlier, an arbitrary length of forty *arpents* was designated for the fields of St. Louis. The origin of this standard dimension is not

---

4. Petition to Congress by Inhabitants of the Territory, St. Louis, Feb. 1, 1806. C. E. Carter, ed. *The Territorial Papers of the United States, Vol. XIII, The Territory of Louisiana-Missouri* (Washington, 1948), 426, 427.

5. "An opinion of the Land Commissioners," c. 1806, Ibid., 499, 501. This policy was also followed, at least in part, at New Madrid. Laforge Memorial, New Madrid, Dec. 20, 1805, Ibid., 409. This does not exactly fit the forty-*arpent* standard of the St. Louis plan.

6. Donaldson to the Secretary of the Treasury, St. Louis, April 26, 1806, Ibid., 494.

7. Cambridge, Mass., etc. 1931.

8. Tours, 1934.

entirely clear. Francis Parkman in *The Old Regime in Canada*[9] stated that the customary length of fields along the St. Lawrence was forty *arpents,* the same as at St. Louis. However, Antoine Roy, provincial archivist of Quebec, comments that "Parkman's affirmation . . . is very hard to prove . . . If the *'Aveux et Denombrements'* were registered to this end, they would demonstrate also that it was far from being the habit. The topography was always taken into account; did it happen, i.e., to exist a river or a stream, a brook or a ravine in the rear of the grant, it served usually as a limit-line in depth. We may say moreover, that the depth of 40 acres *(arpents)* was less than one of 25 or 30 acres."[10]

The first Louisiana land law promulgated by an edict of Louis XV at Paris, October 12, 1716, ordered that land be conceded "in the proportion of two to four *arpents* front by forty to sixty in depth."[11] This is the first mention of *forty* arpents used as a standard. The field length of forty *arpents* was used again at Detroit as early as 1747.[12]

A clause in the land laws published by Don Alexander O'Reilly, Spanish governor of Louisiana, while it did not fit the St. Louis situation exactly, is worth noting: "There shall be granted to each newly arrived family who may wish to establish themselves on the borders of the river six or eight *arpents* in front (according to the means of the cultivator) by forty *arpents* in depth, in order that they may have the benefit of the cypress wood, which is as necessary as useful to the inhabitants."[13] A similar law was published by Intendent Morales in 1799.[14] In 1803 it was stated that the typical grant along the Mississippi "almost invariably expresses a depth of forty acres."[15]

EARLY MILLS

T HE PRIMITIVE MILLS used in the old French villages across the river from St. Louis were described by John Reynolds:

---

9. 1902 ed., II: 50.

10. Letter to the author, Dec. 15, 1947. Three of the earliest grants of land in the Illinois Country were those made by La Salle in 1683 from his seigneury on the Illinois River. Their dimensions were:

   (D'Autrey grant) 126 *arpents* front x 42 *arpents* depth

   (Prudhomme grant) 44 *arpents* front x 44 *arpents* depth

   (Disy grant) 10 *arpents* front x 33⅓ *arpents* depth

Theodore C. Pease, *The French Foundations, 1680-1693* (Springfield, 1934), 19, 28, 29, 33, 43.

11. *Louisiana Historical Quarterly,* 14 (July 1931): 347.

12. ASP: PL I: 306.

13. Ibid., IV: 3.

14. Ibid., III: 488.

15. ASP., Miscellaneous, I: 350.

In early times, these various expedients were resorted to by the people to manufacture corn meal. The band mill was so called because a twisted rawhide band was put on the large wheel, in the place of cogs. It saved the gearing of the mill. They are the lowest and cheapest order of horse mills. Pins are put in the arms of the large wheel, and around them the band is placed. These pins may be changed into holes, made for the purpose; so the band may be made tighter, when necessary.

The next is the hand mill. The stones are smaller than those of the horse mill and propelled by man or woman power. A hole is made in the upper stone, and a staff of wood is put in it, and the other end of the staff is put through a hole in a plank above, so that the whole is free to act. One or two persons take hold of this staff and turn the upper stone with as much velocity as possible. An eye is made in the upper stone, thro' which the corn is put into the mill, with the hand, in small quantities, to suit the mill, instead of a hopper. This is a hand mill.[16]

The public baking of bread in Spanish Louisiana was such an essential activity that a baker appeared on the government payrolls of most towns. Indian allies seem to have been fed regularly and official reports were made of the bread and corn thus consumed.[17] In the fort at New Madrid there was a government bakery[18] but at St. Louis the provisioning of the garrison and the Indians with bread and crackers was contracted for through public bidding.[19] In the early years Laclède, the founder and principal merchant, was allowed 600 *livres* per year in lieu of a government baker.[20]

The high value of milling and baking in the St. Louis colonial economy was proven by the award to Manuel Lisa of a five-year monopoly of the rich Osage Indian fur trade for the consideration of building a watermill and donation of $1,000. This mill, with " . . . two runs of stones . . . as well equipped as those of the Anglo-Americans . . ." was actually built in 1802 or 1803.[21] Its location is not certain; it was probably on the tract of land owned by Lisa about this time, which was south of St. Louis near the old Peoria Indian village.[22] The records show that

---

16. Reynolds, 144.

17. E.g., the report on this subject for the years 1770 and 1771 was among the official papers returned to New Orleans by Delassus in 1804. See inventory, Delassus Papers, Missouri Historical Society.

18. Carondelet to Delassus, New Orleans, March 28, 1797. Ibid.

19. Morales to Delassus, New Orleans, May 5, 1803. Ibid.

20. A. P. Nasatir, "Government Employees and Salaries in Spanish Louisiana," *Louisiana Historical Quarterly,* 29 (October 1946): 32.

21. Petition of March 14, 1803, signed "Manuel de Lisa y Compañia."

22. The land, of unspecified size, was described as "a Plantation situated about a league below this town" between the Mississippi and the road to Carondelet. It was bounded on the south by

Lisa's plans also included the making of bread, for in 1800 he made a contract with a baker named Juan Gatzoza,[23] and in 1803 he bought the old Barrera bakery with all its equipment.[24] The success of this enterprise is not known; it undoubtedly ended with all the other Spanish trading monompolies in 1804 when the Americans took over.

BUILDING THE CHURCH

THE FRENCH AND SPANISH DOCUMENTS in the collections of the Missouri Historical Society have hardly begun to be exploited. Among them there are several which relate to the building of the second St. Louis church and the adjoining priest's house. These give us an idea of how such public works were handled in the administrations of Piernas and Cruzat.

On December 25 or 26, 1774, the townsmen met and pledged themselves to build a new wooden church to succeed the temporary structure then in use. The following April 19 (the same day as the Battle of Lexington that touched off the Revolutionary War in the East), bids were taken for one of *poteaux en terre* construction, 30' x 60', with a porch six feet wide all around and a lean-to ten feet wide across the rear. Among other features, the specifications called for a large entrance doorway with a round *"oeuil de bouc"* window[25] in the gable above, fourteen other windows of large size, a belfry in the form of a St. Andrew's cross, board floor and ceiling, and a six foot *jubé* or gallery inside with a stairway to reach it. The townsmen pledged themselves to furnish promptly the nails, other ironwork, and the *bouzillage*, as well as to help the contrac-

---

the *petite village sauvage* and north by a brook, possibly the one which turned the mill. This property was bought by Lisa in 1799 from John Rice Jones of Kaskaskia for $201.00 and sold in 1804 to James Berry and Patrick Collins for $800.00. In the meantime it was taken over by one James Cochran who later abandoned it to hunt on the Meramec River. STLRA, 2/3/467, 2/3/511, 2/3/560, and 4/1/16.

23. Gatzoza on May 29, 1800, was engaged for one year. "Under the terms of the contract, Juan does not have to provide wood for the oven, just make good bread. His salary is 400 *pesos* in current coin of the locality, out of which he is to buy his own drink, clothes, and other needs. If he buys them against his pay from Lisa's store he is to be charged regular prices . . . Lisa does provide him at once with a shirt and a pair of buckskins for his work." Sister Mary Hubert McNally, "Manuel Lisa a Pioneer Saint Louisan," (M.A. thesis, St. Louis University, 1945), 46.

24. Purchased October 30, 1803. STLRA, 2/3/527.

25. Literally translated, "goat's eye." The Cahokia church (built c. 1786-1799) had one of these and its framing can still be seen. It is interesting to note the same feature, similarly placed, called an "ox-eye" window, in a 1753 specification for Christ Church, a brick structure still standing in Lancaster County, Virginia. *Virginia Magazine of History and Biography,* 54 (April 1946): 149.

tor raise the heavy timbers. The latter was to provide all the skilled workmen that might be needed (these must be paid promptly) and to complete the work in a manner approved by competent inspectors within a specified time—or be penalized. Pierre Lupien *dit* Baron, St. Louis joiner, bid in the job for 1,200 *livres* in deerskins, and at sunset of the same day—there being no other bidders—got the contract.

The new priest's house, to be built of stone, required the work of two different trades and the procedure followed in this case was more elaborate. On September 1, 1776, the townsmen met to consider the project. It was decided that the *maison curiale* or *presbiterale,* as it was written in the record, should be built of stone laid up in mud mortar, 27′ x 38′ with a ten-foot lean-to across one end, using as far as possible the wood-work from the old house. The work was to go ahead the following spring and Father Bernard himself offered to contribute 437 *livres* in peltries. The agreement was carefully recorded as a *"process dassemblee."*

Final action was not taken, however, until the following summer. The townsmen met again on June 15, 1777, this time at the *Chambre du Governement.* The project was divided into three contracts; one for the masonry, another for furnishing the lumber, and a third for the joinery. The specifications are the most complete we now have for any St. Louis house of the colonial period.

The masonry part called for a house of given size, height, and wall thicknesses, and enumerated the openings for doors and windows. The contractor *(entrepreneur)* was to furnish all the tools, pickaxes, spades, barrels, rakes, mortar, and whitewash, and have the building ready for the roof by the following September 8. The penalty for running over the time limit was 200 *livres.* Should the contractor abandon the project entirely, all the completed work would be forfeit. Sickness of the contractor (confirmed by the town surgeon) would be the only acceptable excuse for delay.

The proposed contract for lumber specified the number and size of doors and windows, the number of framing members, the spacing of rafters, etc. Among other items there are mentioned two runs of steps to the entrance doors, three mantlepieces and the requirement that the shingles be nailed on. Jean B. Cambas, carpenter and joiner, estimated the cost at 2,000 *livres.*

The joinery specification lists eight plain doors, single and double, and eight windows with shutters, and, among other things, called for the installation of the hardware. The work, which was to be carried forward as fast as progress on the masonry permitted, was estimated at 2000 *livres.*

The three proposals were advertised simultaneously on three succeeding Sundays in the customary way. On June 15, at the sound of
the church bell, Francois Cottin, the town crier *(huissier royal),* called
for bids as the townsmen emerged from Mass. The specifications were
read "in a loud clear voice" to those assembled, but there were no bidders. The announcement was repeated on June 22, when two bids were
offered. On June 29 the contracts were awarded as follows: for masonry,
to Benito Vasquez (a merchant trader) for 1,400 *livres* in peltry; for
lumber, to François Delain (master carpenter) for 1,500 *livres* and for
joinery, to Joseph Verdon (joiner) for 299 *livres.*

These structures were actually built and stood well into the American
period.

WORKS OF DEFENSE

A SET OF INTERESTING DOCUMENTS, contributed to the *American
Historical Review* by Professor Lawrence Kinnaird of the University of
California, gives us a picture of the military situation of St. Louis at
the beginning of the American Revolution. In 1778 friendly cor-
respondence between Gov. Patrick Henry of Virginia and the Spanish
Governor Galvez of Louisiana bore fruit in close cooperation between
the Spanish lieutenant governor at St. Louis, Fernando de Leyba, Col.
George Rogers Clark at Kaskaskia, and Capt. Joseph Bowman at nearby
Cahokia. Leyba welcomed the Virginians with salutes and entertained
them generously, even giving dances their first two nights in town.[26]
Supplies for Clark's Illinois regiment were provided by St. Louisans
in a sort of "cold war" against the British.

Early in 1779, however, Leyba was warned that British spies had been
at St. Louis to gather information on his defenses. Reporting this to
New Orleans, he wrote:

> The affair has me somewhat on the alert. Sixteen men including the
> drummer are all the troops I have with me and I hardly have forty
> of the militiamen capable of bearing arms since at this season they are
> all trading on the Misury, hunting, or in that place [New Orleans].
> Although the barracks are of stone they would be little protection since
> their parts are not protected by one another. Neither can we from within
> prevent the enemy from approaching its walls and they could make
> the breach there and to enter without the slightest risk. If the attack

---

26. Leyba to Galvez, St. Louis, Nov. 16, 1778, *American Historical Review,* 4 (October 1935):
102. "There was a great consuming of powder at his arrival as well as at his departure."

which he directs at Colonel Clark were only by royalist troops, there would not be the least fear, but the practice in Indian wars is to attack not where one should be but where there is the least risk.[27]

A generation later, at the end of the colonial period, Perrin du Lac, a French traveler in Upper Louisiana, wrote that the St. Louis military establishment included "the garrison, which does not exceed sixty men, a galley which employs twenty-four oarsmen and the military hospital . . ."[28] Little is known about the latter, except that it had a surgeon and that, due to the healthy climate of St. Louis (according to Spanish accounts), it had few patients.[29]

Among the causes contributing to the final ruin of the fortifications was a tornado which visited St. Louis the night of April 3, 1803, and took off the roof of the barracks and armory.[30] Within a year, however, everything was turned over to the American troops under Captain Stoddard. During the Indian scares of the fall and winter of 1804 the old fortifications were hastily repaired against a rumored invasion[31] but in the following year Cantonment Bellefontaine on the Missouri River was garrisoned and it superseded St. Louis as a military outpost.

EARLY ENGINEERS

O F CHARLES WARIN, the young engineer and artist who visited St. Louis with General Collot in 1796, we have a description in the early counterintelligence files of the American army. He was mentioned by James McHenry as "lately a sub-engineer in the service of the United States, which he resigned for his present employment, speaks English tolerably, is about thirty years of age, about six feet high, black hair, ruddy complexion, and easy manners."[32]

In the early territorial documents the work of Antoine Soulard, another of the six engineers of colonial St. Louis, is revealed in greater detail then previously known. Soulard, who had been an officer of the French Navy,[33] left the old country about the time of the great revolution to try his fortune in the New World. Somehow he got to St. Louis and

---

27. Leyba to Galvez, St. Louis, Feb. 5, 1779, Ibid., 105.

28. Perrin du lac, *Voyage dans les Deux Louisianes*, (Lyon, 1805), 189.

29. Morales to Delassus, New Orleans, Nov. 5, 1802, Delassus Papers.

30. Morales to Delassus, New Orleans, April 28, 1803, and Salcedo to Delassus, New Orleans, May 3, 1803. Delassus Papers.

31. James Bruff to James Wilkinson, St. Louis, Sept. 29, Nov. 5, 1804, March 12, 1805. Carter, *Territorial Papers, Louisiana-Missouri*, 60, 79, 101-03.

32. William Henry Smith, ed., *St. Clair Papers*, Cincinnati, 1882, II: 395, 396.

33. Carter, Territorial papers, Louisiana-Missouri, 526.

on February 3, 1795, he was appointed surveyor general of Upper Louisiana[34] with headquarters at St. Louis. For field work he received four *sous* per acre or three *reales* per day, exclusive of traveling expenses.[35] The colonial archives still contain many of his neat pen-and-ink plats and the map of St. Louis of about 1804 illustrated in this essay seems also to have been his work.

When the St. Louis fortifications were augmented under Don Carlos Howard and Louis Vanden Bemden, Soulard assisted by drawing up the plans. He was warmly commended for this work, which he performed under the title of adjutant-major, pro tem. ''His talents, liberal education and cultivated acquirements'' were cited in a recommendation for a permanent commission.[36] In the year 1800, although not considered an ''engineer,'' Soulard was acknowledged by the Spanish staff at New Orleans to be very capable and he was entrusted to the job of supervising the repair of the fort at St. Louis.[37] Soulard was a fine draftsman and enjoyed a reputation as a man of honor and probity.[38] After the change of government in 1804 he was continued at reduced compensation for nearly two years as territorial surveyor, but finally lost out in the bitter politics of the times.[39]

Other sources will soon bring us new information on colonial St. Louis. The National Park Service, through the Library of Congress, is procuring on microfilm from Spanish archives the unpublished letters and reports of St. Ange de Bellerive, St. Louis' first commandant. Three volumes of Spanish colonial documents, many of which relate to Upper Louisiana, are in press for Professor Laurence Kinnaird of the University of California. A volume of documents pertaining to Cahokia will be published by the St. Louis Historical Documents Foundation under the editorship of Professor John Francis McDermott in May 1949. Two more volumes of documents relating to colonial affairs on the Mississippi and Missouri rivers are in preparation by Dr. A. P. Nasatir of San Diego for the Documents Foundation.

Charles E. Peterson.

Richmond, Virginia

March 15, 1949

34. Ibid., 523.

35. Ibid., 436.

36. Ibid., 532, 533. Certificate of Carlos Howard, St. Louis, Aug. 1, 1797. (The original, which seems to have been in error, read 1796.)

37. Lopez y Angula to Delassus, New Orleans, March 22, 1800, Delassus Papers.

38. J. B. C. Lucas to Secretary of the Treasury, Pittsburgh, June 25, 1804. Ibid., 26.

39. Ibid., 71, 72, 433, 536. In an article ''Observation on certain Parts of the Country in Louisiana,'' dated March 1805, published in the *English Monthly Magazine* 23 (March 1, 1807): 124-127, Soulard claimed to have personally ascended the Missouri River 1,800 miles. As territorial surveyor he was succeeded by Silas Bent of Ohio in 1806.

A New Supplement
of Ilustrations

WHEN THIS LITTLE BOOK WAS FIRST PUBLISHED SERIALLY IN 1947—under the leadership of the late Charles van Ravenswaay— Missouri Historical Society funds did not allow the use of many pictures. Today, editor Gregory M. Franzwa of The Patrice Press has encouraged me to add some images collected over the years from such historically related areas as French Canada, France itself, the shores of the Gulf of Mexico, and the Caribbean, especially islands first settled by the French. So here are additional illustrations revealing precedent for the distinctive building types of the Illinois Country French. They are quite different from those brought by the Anglo-Americans late to the Mississippi Valley.

Some of these examples first appeared in my contribution, "The French Houses of Colonial St. Louis," in John Francis McDermott, ed., *The French in the Mississippi Valley* (University of Illinois Press, 1965).

Over the years numbers of illustrated volumes have been published on the vernacular architecture of both France and French Canada. I have made no attempt to consult them all. But here are some examples: Georges Doyon and Robert Hubrecht, *L'Architecture Rurale & Bourgeoise en France* (Paris, 1967) and Bill Laws, *Traditional Houses of Rural France* (New York, London, Paris, 1991). For French Canada: *Commission des Monuments Historiques de la Province de Québec, Vieux Manoirs, Vielles Maisons* (Quebec, 1927). Michael Lessard and Huguette Marquis, *Encyclopédie de la Maison Quebecoise, 33 Siecles de'Habitations* (Montreal, 1972), and Peter Moogk, *Building a Home in New France* (Toronto, 1979). Considering the burst of courage and energy it took to establish frontier St. Louis, the pictorial record is today pitifully scarce. Well over one hundred years ago the last colonial structure was pulled down. But we do have recourse to the survivors in old Ste. Genevieve to the south on the right bank of the Mississippi. Taken together with the St. Louis Recorded Archives so abundantly quoted in this book, I hope the reader can somehow visualize the little metropolis that soon proved to be the Gateway to the West.

Charles E. Peterson

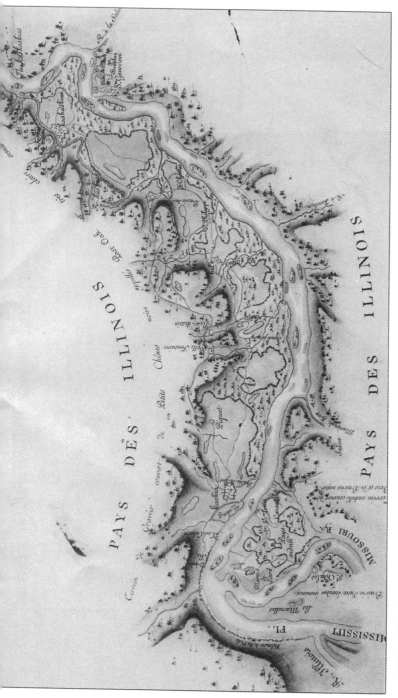

"The Illinois Country," according to Gen. Victor Collot (north to the left), lay between what today are the states of Illinois (top) and Missouri. This map depicts the Mississippi River in 1796 from the Missouri, gateway to the rich fur trade—down to LaSaline Creek, a valuable source of salt. On the west bank were located the villages (starting from the right) of (New) Bourbon, Ste. Genevieve, Carondelet, St. Louis, and St. Charles. On the east bank may be seen Kaskaskia, Fort Chartres, Prairie du Rocher, St. Phillipe, Prairie duPont, and Cahokia. *Vincennes, Service Historique de la Marine, Carte No. 7, courtesy Elizabeth Starr Cummin.*

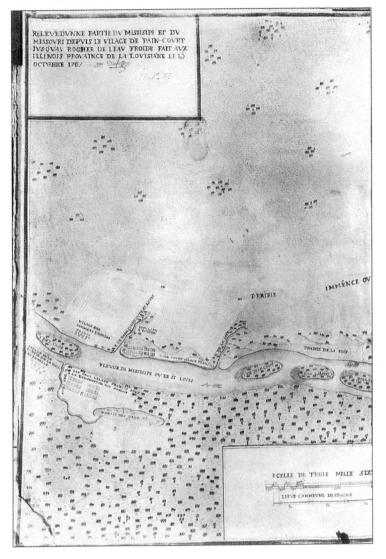

This 1767 map, signed by engineer Guy Dufossat, is entitled *"RELEVE D'UNNE PARTIE DU MISSISSIPPI ET DU MISSOURI DEPUIS LE VILAGE DE PAIN-COURT IUSQUAU ROCHER DE LEAU FROIDE."* The new town of St. Louis, shown in a diagrammatic way, is labelled *"PAIN-COURT VILAGE FRANÇOIS."* Just below is the *"R[IVIERE] DE PAINCOURT OU DE ST. LOUIS"*—now a nearly forgotten stream covered over in Mill Creek Valley—and Joseph Tayon's watermill. *From a print in the Lowery Collection, Maps Division, Library of Congress, Washington. Original in the Biblioteca Nacional, Madrid.*

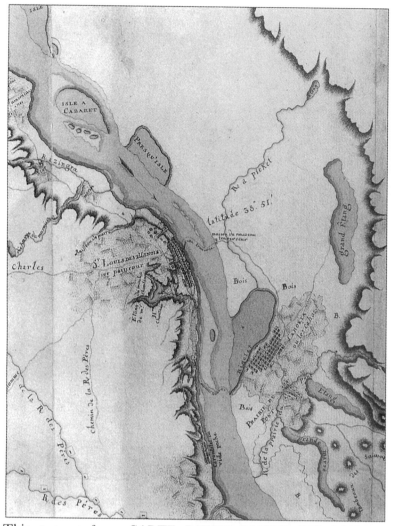

This excerpt from *CARTE D'UNE PARTIE DU COURS DU MISSISSIPPI... LEVÉE ET DESTINNEE PENDANT LE COURS 1797 ET 1798 D^N NICHOLAS DE FINIELS, INGENIEUR EXTRRE*, shows St. Louis, Cahokia, and the vicinity. De Finiels, a French engineer commissioned by the Spanish minister at Philadelphia, arrived in St. Louis in 1797. His map provides details—from St. Cyr's establishment on Gingrass Creek (with Americans uproad) down to Carondelet (*Vide Poche*) and the Indian mounds (*Tombeaux des Sauvages*) below Prairie Dupont on the east bank of the Mississippi.

Two ferry crossings from St. Louis to the old village of Cahokia (or *les Cahos*) up Rigolet Creek are indicated: the *"ancienne traverse"* skirted a sand bar, the *"nouvelle traverse"* landed at the *"maison du Nouveau traverseur,"* presumably a ferryman's house. *Service Historique de la Marine, Vincennes, courtesy Elizabeth Starr Cummin.*

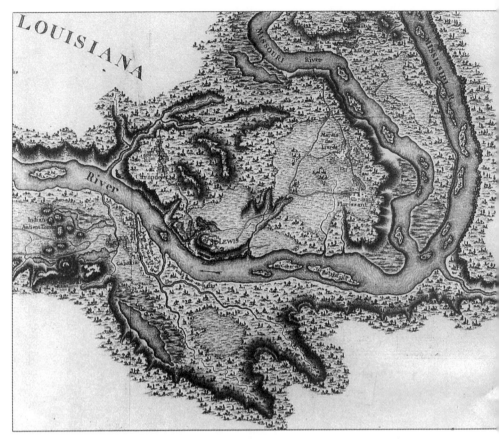

This excerpt from a 1796 English version of *CARTE PARTICULIERE des Cours DU MISSISSIPI Pour Service L' inteligence du Voyage DU GENERAL COLLOT*, contains inaccuracies but records interesting details for the first time. The engraved map shows the old road leading northwest from St. Louis. It reached Florissant (established in April 1787) in the parish of St. Ferdinand, *Marais des Liards* (Cottonwood Swamp, currently Bridgeton), and finally St. Charles (townsite surveyed in 1787) on the left bank of the Missouri River. Opposite the mouth of the latter is Wood River, where Lewis and Clark would soon encamp, preparing for their celebrated expedition to the Pacific Ocean. North is to the right. *Collot Ensemble, 71 Recueil 66. Service Historique de la Marine, courtesy Elizabeth Starr Cummin.*

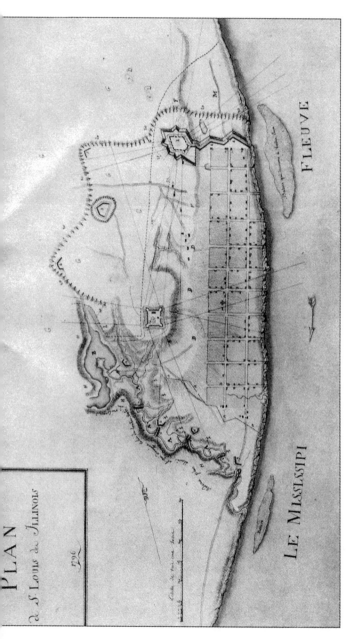

PLAN
a S. Louis des Illinois

1796

LE MISSISSIPI

FLEUVE

Collot's large scale "*PLAN de S. Louis des Illinois, 1796,*" is one of several contemporary versions of the St. Louis townsite. It depicts many details for the first time. The palisaded Fort San Carlos with its stone tower (a *cavalier* was erected in 1781) had been built just in time to oppose the grand attack of British and Indians. However, some of the features shown were only proposals for fortifying the town and were never carried out. Rocky ledges on the river-bank are clearly indicated. In the river may be seen two sandbars (*batures*) exposed at low water.

The streets were laid out regularly, dividing the town into blocks. These, in turn, were generally divided into four building lots (*emplacements*). The unbuilt square on the river-bank was the *Place d'Armes*, the parish church was the cross-shaped structure in the center. Probably drawn by Charles Warin, General Collot's adjutant. *Service Historique de la Marine, Vincennes, courtesy Elizabeth Starr Cummin.*

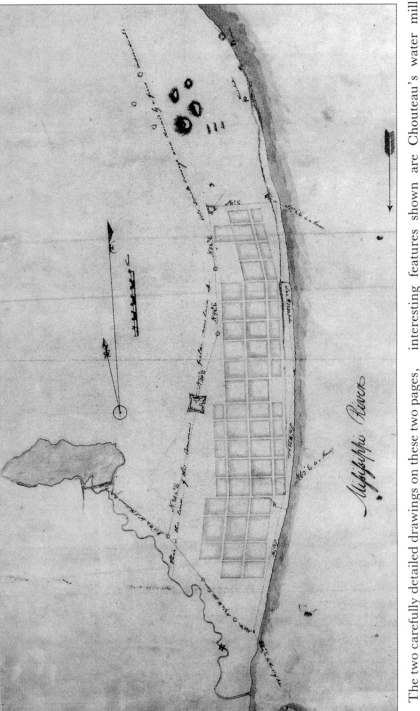

The two carefully detailed drawings on these two pages, ca. 1804, are both entitled "Map of the Mississippi Country." They seem to be in the draftsmanship of the surveyor Antoine Soulard. Besides the fortifications around the town, interesting features shown are Chouteau's water mill (formerly Tayon's) with nearby orchard and distillery, Motard's and Roy's windmills, the calvary on the hill, several Indian mounds and roads leading to to neighbor-

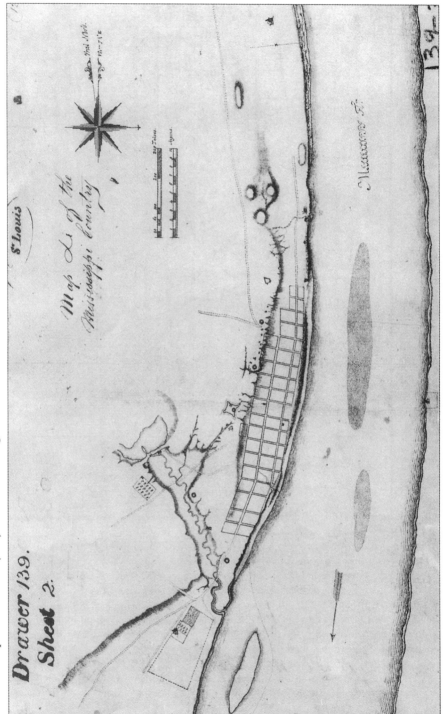

ng settlements. The two maps, more or less contemporary, supplement rather than contradict each other. They were clearly made using up-to-date surveying instruments. Note on the compass rose true (*vrai*) north and magnetic north.

of the Mississippi River. Originals from the U.S. Army Corps of Engineers, now in the National Archives.

Drawer 139. Sheet 2.

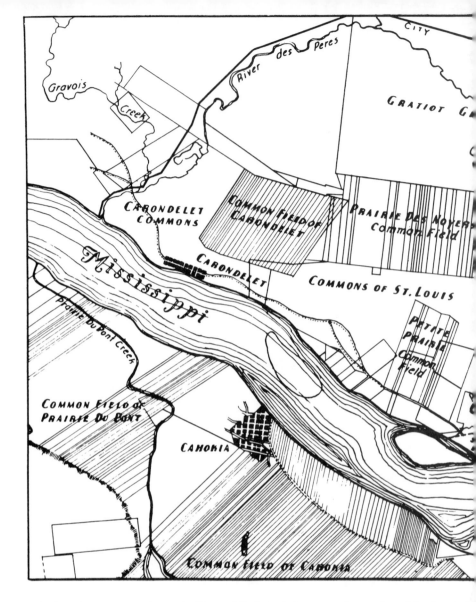

When the French came to settle on the Upper Mississippi there was plenty of good land and the chose open prairies for cultivation rather than clear the forests. These prairies were laid off into lor narrow strips, as were the fields of medieval Europe and French Canada. The unit of measure wa the *arpent*, or "Paris acre." Most fields were one or two *arpents* wide. At Cahokia, a settlement bega in 1699, the fields ran across the bottomlands from a channel of the Mississippi to the bluffs on th east. At St. Louis, founded in 1764, there were no such natural boundaries and an arbitrary lengt of forty *arpents* was used. "St. Louis Prairie," "Grand Prairie," and the "Prairie des Noyers" we the principal cultivated areas. The lands of colonial St. Louis extended over twenty-five square mil before the new settlement was five years old.

Instead of fencing these strips individually, whole tracts were protected by a common enclosure, th upkeep of which was subdivided among the proprietors and supervised by *syndics* elected at speci assemblies.

he Illinois country villages were built compactly for better defense asnd the farmers lived alongside
other citizens. The commonfields system was maintained at St. Louis until the later 1790s, when
warlike Osage nation was pacified and the white population spread out. The great fences were then
adoned in favor of the Anglo-American practice of individual farming. At Cahokia, where French
itions lasted longer, the common fence was maintained into the nineteenth century.
he location of St. Louis streets is still dominated by the eighteenth century pattern of the plowlands.
instance, the bent west boundary of St. Louis Prairie is today Jefferson Avenue, and the west boun-
of the Prairie des Noyers field is South Kingshighway. The shorelines of the river have changed
ion a number of times since history began here and the islands have disappeared altogether. This
, based on the 1848 Hutawa Atlas, was redrawn by Frank R. Leslie of the staff of the Jefferson
onal Expansion Memorial.

The fourth edition (1786) of *La Nouvelle Maison Rustique ou Économie Generale* was published in Paris during the colonial period of St. Louis. Its two volumes were evidently intended for use by country gentlemen, having hints for ornamental fountains and the upper-class pursuit of game. But the plates reproduced on this and the succeeding three pages offer pictures of the French peasant at work, his lands and his tools. The scenes could as easily have been in colonial St. Louis. *Author's library.*

Sowing Grain

Eighteenth century agricultural equipment of rural France.

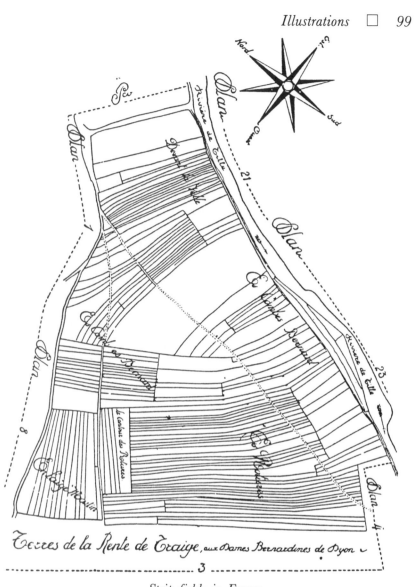

Strip fields in France

Dr. Emmanuel LeRoy Ladurie of the Bibliotheque Nationale states that ancient long and narrow strip fields like those on the St. Lawrence and the Mississippi could be found earlier in the east of France, especially in Lorraine and the Vosges, as well as in nearby Germany and Switzerland. This map is from Marc Bloch, *Les Caracteres Originaux de l'Histoire Rural Francaise*, Oslo, 1931, Planche VI. The plowlands shown abut the Riviere de Tille in the Cote d'Or near Dijon. *Van Pelt Library, University of Pennsylvania.*

Partial View of St. Louis

A St. Louis banknote, engraved by Leney and Rollinson of New York, carries this ca. 1815 view of the town from the water. The earliest printed view known, it was evidently made from a crude sketch about a dozen years after the close of the colonial period. Identifiable buildings are the Laclede-Chouteau House (upper left), the public market house on the town square and the round stone tower fort on the skyline (built 1780). *Collection of Eric P. Newman, St. Louis.*

High and dry above the Mississippi, the site selected for Laclede's St. Louis was defended by steep limestone ledges. This is believed to be the first publication of this light pencil sketch, rendered in 1826 by the French artist/naturalist Charles Alexandre Lesueur (1778-1846). It offers an idea of the original topography. In 1818 Manuel Lisa, the celebrated fur trader, built his little warehouse on a ledge at the foot of Chestnut Street; part of one floor was only naked rock. The structure was first carefully restored—and then demolished—during the development of the Jefferson National Expansion Memorial. *Musée d'Histoire Naturelle, LeHavre.*

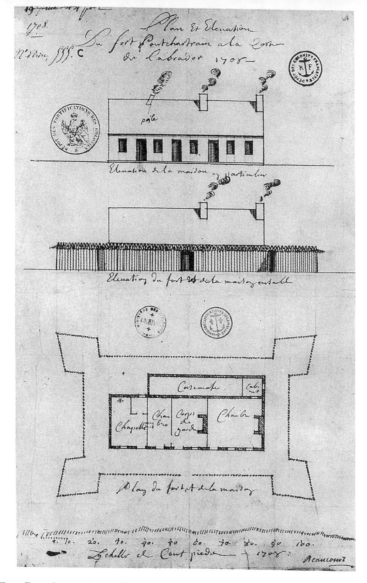

Fort Ponchartrain, a diminuitive French post on the coast of Labrador, was built in 1708. Close set walls of sharpened pickets served well enough as protection against Indian attack by bow and arrow or small arms. This was the common type of enclosure across America's frontiers, when timber was easily available. In the Illinois Country villages each house lot was typically surrounded by such an enclosure. The palisades did not last long and needed replacement in about four years. Red cedar and white mulberry were the most durable species. Note the stove (*poele*) and stovepipe shared by the chapel and a bedroom (*chambre*). Iron stoves were being freighted up the river to St. Louis from New Orleans as early as 1798. Image stamped *"DEPOT DES FORTIFICATIONS DES COLONIES"* and *"DEPOT DES COLONIES FRANCAISES RF"*

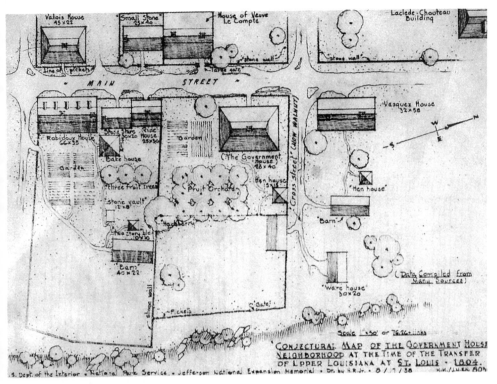

This map depicting St. Louis town lots as of 1804 was compiled from many documentary sources by Henry E. Rice, Jr., National Park Service landscape draftsman. It shows the various improvements in the vicinity of Government House, where the surrender of Upper Louisiana took place on "Three Flags Day," March 10, 1804. The drawing was prepared for the makers of a diorama still on display in the Jefferson National Expansion Memorial. The favorite species for such palisades (upright pickets, or *pieux*) was the red cedar (*Juniperus virginiana*). That tree finally became so scarce that logs had to be imported from a great distance up the Missouri River. *Jefferson National Expansion Memorial Archives.*

This pen and ink drawing of an American Indian house c. 1540 was used by Fernandez de Oviedo y Valdes in his *Historia Natural y General de las Indias*. Depicted is a structure of spaced upright posts set in the earth and connected with curtain walls of slender poles bound with vines. The thatch would likely have been of palm fronds or grass. This image is out of drawing but is important as likely the earliest known picture of a native house in the New World. *Huntington Library, San Marino, Cal.*

This thatched post house stands near Gonaïve, Haiti. Such structures are still being built generally in North Haiti, by descendants of French slaves. *Author, 1961.*

This *jacal,* or Mexican hut, recently stood in San Antonio, Texas. Such houses, with palisaded walls, were not uncommon in nineteenth-century Texas and may have been a heritage from the local Indians. *Old stereoptican view provided by Marvin Eichenroht, AIA.*

The Bequet-Ribault House, on St. Mary's Road in Ste. Genevieve, Missouri, is one of three *poteaux en terre* structures in that city. The red cedar logs of the exterior walls were hewn flat above grade but left in the round below. Through the years the clay *bousillage* has been tunneled by wasps. *Author, 1937.*

The Bienvenue House stood on the northwest corner of Third and Plum streets in St. Louis. Built in 1786 and demolished in 1875, the 20' x 25' house originally had a *galerie* on all sides and probably a tall pavillon roof. Its ruined condition shows the palisaded wall construction (*poteaux en terre*) characteristic of most eighteenth-century houses of the Illinois Country. Farther south, in the French Carribbean and in Mayan territory on the mainland, *poteaux en terre* houses of lighter construction are still being built. *From a daguerreotype by Thomas M. Easterly, ca. 1850, courtesy of Missouri Historical Society.*

The Jacques Noisé House (before 1780), was on the northwest corner of Main and Spruce Streets in St. Louis. Shown here in ruins, the
structure is known from the land records to have been a *poteaux en terre*
building, 22' x 30', with a *galerie* on three sides. Alexander McNair,
first governor of Missouri, owned the property for about thirteen years.
*From a daguerreotype by Thomas M. Easterly, ca. 1850s, courtesy of Missouri
Historical Society.*

Isolated in northwest St. Louis County across the Missouri River from St. Charles, this house was said to have been built with horizontal logs. It has long been gone. Identified sometimes as ''Fort Bonfils'' and sometimes as ''Old Chouteau Mansion,'' it displays many typical features such as an all-around *galerie* and a hipped roof with an *epi* (tuft) at the apex where the shingles met. The curved-top, double-hung windows were unusual and indicate a late-date, Anglo-American influence. *Photographed ca. 1871 by Robert Goebel, courtesy of Missouri Historical Society.*

Horizontal hewn logs were dropped between vertical posts channeled to receive them, to form the walls of this house in St. Placide, Quebec. The logs were pegged in places, but no spikes or nails were used. This is probably an example of what has been called the "Montreal" or "Red River frame." An alternative type of construction involved logs alternating with the corners dovetailed *(en queue d'hironde.) Author, 1939.*

The log wall details may be seen clearly in this 1879 photograph of "Fort Misery," actually the Hudson's Bay Company's Fort McLeod, British Columbia. This construction type had crossed the whole width of Canada. *Photographer unknown, Geological Survey of Canada.*

The Dodier-Sarpy House (1766?), on the northeast corner of Second and Clark streets in St. Louis, displayed a roof form which was typical of the colonial period. The framed wing is probably a kitchen. The house was owned by the widow of Manuel Lisa for more than forty years. *Photographer unknown. Courtesy Missouri Historical Society.*

The Lorraine-Lisa House (before 1799), stood on the southwest corner of Second and Spruce streets. This view shows typical glazed French doors, but the windows are double-hung instead of the usual early hinged casements which swung in. The house probably was built for Jean Baptiste Lorraine, a tanner. It was sold by him to Lisa in 1799. *Photographer unknown, courtesy Missouri Historical Society.*

The old village of Cahokia still exists across the Mississippi from St. Louis. It was founded as a mission to the Tamaroa Indians by seminarians from Quebec. Established in 1699, it is almost a generation older than New Orleans.

Two of Cahokia's French houses lasted into the age of photography. The so-called Cahokia Courthouse, also known as the Saucier House, is of *colombage* construction and is probably older than the town of St. Louis. In 1893 it was moved to Chicago and exhibited as a historical curiosity on an island at the Columbian Exposition. Four decades later it was moved back to its original site and reconstructed by the state of Illinois. *Photographed by Jacob Siler in 1904. Courtesy Missouri Historical Society.*

Cahokia's Droitz House was in decrepit condition in 1893 when it was photographed by Emil Boehl of St. Louis. It reveals heavy French walls filled with stone, whitewashed and later covered with hand-split lath and probably plastered again. No sill is visible; the verticals may have been planted in the ground *(poteaux en terre). Courtesy Missouri Historical Society*.

The *poteaux* forming the walls of the Lamarque House in Old Mines, Mo., are mortised and pegged to the plate. The sides of the posts were hacked to retain *bouzillage. Author, 1937.*

In Ste. Genevieve's famed Bolduc House, the *poteaux* are spiked to the plate and the interstices filled in with *bouzillage*. Note the unique log floor of the attic. *Author, 1937.*

The puncheon floor of the attic of the Herbst House, in Florissant, Mo., may be seen below the *poteaux* as they meet the hand-hewn plate. The stone filling is loose; it may have been laid in mud which later leached out. *Author, 1937.*

In Normandy timber was available for building well into the eighteenth century. The frames of these very old *colombage* houses in Rouen on the Seine were filled with stone *(pierrotage)*. A large number were lost, possibly including these, when in World War II, a German tank caught fire and destroyed a large area. *Author, 1938.*

Colombage bouzillée is exposed in this barn near Evreux, Normandy. The word *bouzillage* comes from the French term for cow dung, which probably was manufactured in quantities inside. Mixed with mud and straw, it was used to fill the frame. *Jack Boucher, 1972.*

The Laclède-Chouteau House was on the west side of First Street, between Market and Walnut, a site which is now part of the Jefferson National Expansion Memorial on the downtown St. Louis riverfront. It was built in 1764, remodeled about 1795, and demolished in 1841. This 1840 lithograph by J. C. Wild appeared in Lewis Foulk Thomas ed., *The Valley of the Mississippi Illustrated*, St. Louis, 1841. This stone building first served as the St. Louis headquarters for Maxent, Laclède & Co. of New Orleans. After standing vacant for several years it was purchased by Auguste Chouteau, first citizen of early St. Louis, and remodeled into the Louisiana-style mansion as shown here. A rough floor plan of this building is shown on page 142. *Courtesy Missouri Historical Society.*

The Pierre Chouteau House was built about 1785 on the west side of Main Street, between Vine and Washington, on what is now the downtown St. Louis riverfront. The large stone structure is shown here in an early painting. It was one of the most elegant houses of the town, its owner a leading fur trader. The artist is identified as Susan Paddock; the year of the painting as 1870, some thirty-five years after the building's demolition. *Courtesy Missouri Historical Society.*

The Robidoux-Sanguinet-Benoist House was built after 1787 by trader Joseph Robidoux. The rock building stood on the northeast corner of Main and Elm streets in St. Louis long enough to be photographed twice. Almost buried between later additions, the French *galerie* and chimneys of the original house can be identified.

Limestone for building was readily available in all the Illinois Country villages. The first stone house was built by Philippe Renault near Fort Chartres in 1723. *Photographer unknown. Courtesy of Missouri Historical Society.*

The stone chimneys of the Robidoux-Sanguinet-Benoist House are of typical French form. In the rear is a two-story stone bakehouse with a steep pyramidal roof. The production of bread and biscuits was an early St. Louis industry which supplied *habitants, voyageurs,* and friendly Indians alike. *Photographer unknown. Courtesy Missouri Historical Society.*

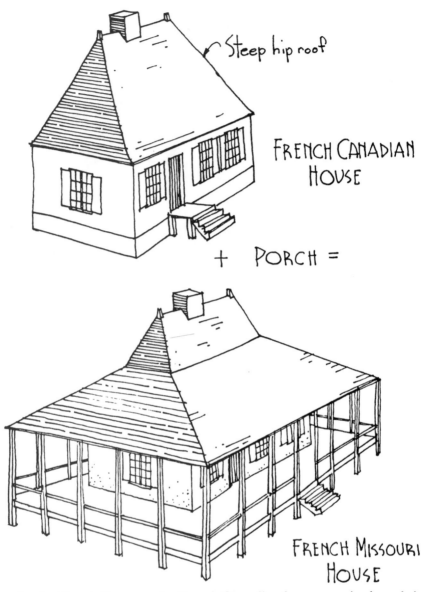

Steep hip roof

FRENCH CANADIAN
HOUSE

+ PORCH =

FRENCH MISSOURI
HOUSE

In the Illinois Country the French Canadian house acquired a *galerie* introduced from the South. Such porches protected the structural walls and were useful for summer living in spite of mosquitoes. But such great roofs were expensive to maintain. In the case of the Bolduc House in Ste. Genevieve, the hewn *galerie* posts rose out of the earth. Below grade many revealed part of the tree's root system. *Drawings by author.*

This model of a typical Illinois Country house was designed by the author after a study of surviving houses and the abundant documentary references. The cutaway parts show the *poteaux en terre,* standing upright in the ground and spiked to a plate at the top. The recently restored Bequet-Ribault house on St. Mary's Road in Ste. Genevieve is a comparable example, the study of which proved very useful. This model was built by the National Park Service Museum Laboratory, Washington, D.C., under the direction of the late Ned J. Burns. It is today displayed in the Old Courthouse at the Jefferson National Expansion Memorial, St. Louis.

The Giroux House, in Charlebourg, Quebec, is a typical small framed Quebec country house, unusually complete as to detail. *Author, 1939.*

The Leveau House, on False River near Chenal, Louisiana, is a remarkably complete small French house similar to those of colonial St. Louis, except that it was mounted high on cypress blocks to keep it from the rising moisture. *Photograph ca. 1919, Richard Koch FAIA.*

This watercolor of a decaying Creole farmhouse is by Elizabeth Von Phul of St. Louis, dated 1818. The location is unknown, but it probably was along the Mississippi or Missouri rivers near St. Louis. *Courtesy of Charles van Ravenswaay and the Missouri Historical Society.*

These kingpost roof trusses are in the Bolduc House at Ste. Genevieve. Note the log floor. *Author, 1937.*

These massive roof trusses are in the Ste. Gemme-Amoreaux House,
St. Mary's Road, Ste Genevieve. *Author, 1937.*

The roof truss system in the Guibourd-Valle House, Fourth Street, Ste. Genevieve, is a popular feature with visitors to the building. The structure is owned by the Ste. Genevieve Foundation and is open to the public. *Author, 1937.*

The roof framing of this country house near Evreux, Normandy, is similar to the trusses used in the Illinois Country. *Jack Boucher, 1972.*

This thatched-roof house near Caumont, Normandy, was falling into ruins when examined. Such roofs, constructed by local artisans, had to have a pitch steep enough to shed rainwater. Once dried out, they were a serious fire hazard and a refuge for vermin. The earliest Ste. Genevieve houses show evidence of roof thatching; some colonial St. Louis structures were so covered. *Author, 1938.*

Heavy timber walls of the house shown on the previous page support pole rafters. Bundles of thatch (of straw, grass, or rushes) are bound to thatching strips by coarse twine. Such roofing was warm and picturesque but liable to infestation by rodents, birds, and insects. *Author, 1938.*

This thatched log barn was in the vicinity of Baie St. Paul, Quebec. *Author, 1939.*

There were at least three windmills in the Illinois Country. One was shown on the Hutchins map of 1766 just north of Kaskaskia. In St. Louis, Motard's wooden mill stood near Fort San Carlos. Roy's stone tower mill stood on the St. Louis riverfront near Mullanphy Street. It was built in 1797 and demolished ca. 1853. Resembling the mills along the St. Lawrence River, it once had a revolving top and sails, probably of canvas. it was the official beginning of St. Louis town limits at the time of incorporation in 1809 and was usually referred to as "Roy's Tower." This is the front view of the tower.

Like the Tayon-Chouteau watermill, Roy's would have ground the flour used in the public bakeries. The Illinois Country served as the breadbasket of the Lower Mississippi and New Orleans. Both these photographs were taken ca. 1850s by Thomas M. Easterly. *Courtesy Missouri Historical Society.*

The Chouquet Stone Tower Mill east of Vercheres, Quebec, is typical of the mills found all along the St. Lawrence River and as far west as Detroit. The wooden tops could be turned into the wind as it changed direction. They were not easy to manage but they served year-around. Waterpower mills, on account of ice, could not operate in the winter. *Author, 1939.*

A rear view of the Chouquet windmill. *Author, 1939.*

The St. Louis antiquarian/annalist Frederic Billon left this pen-and-ink sketch of what was probably the main floor arrangement in St. Louis's first permanent structure. Presumably it depicts the layout as remodeled by Auguste Chouteau for his private residence. It omits the *galeries* that surrounded the house. *Frederic L. Billon papers, Missouri Historical Society.*

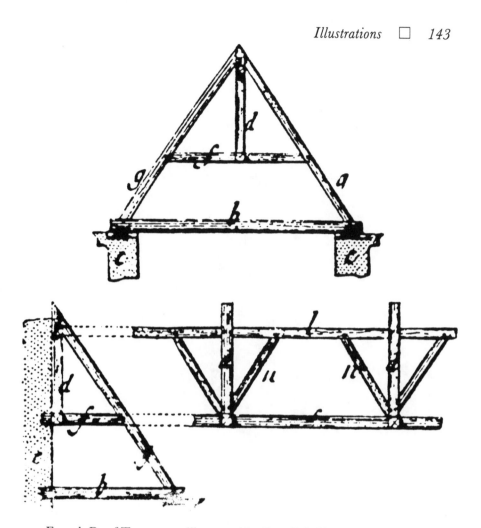

French Roof Trusses, as illustrated in *Recueil de Planches de l'Enclycopédie*, Paris, 1783.

A full complement of fittings is shown in this doorway of a stone house at St. Sylvain, Normandy. Note shutters (*contrevents*) opening out. They are held together with tapering, dovetailed battens and iron strap hinges hung on pintles driven into the door frame. Jib doors swing in with hinged, glazed casements. The same features could be found in early houses along the Mississippi. *Author, 1938.*

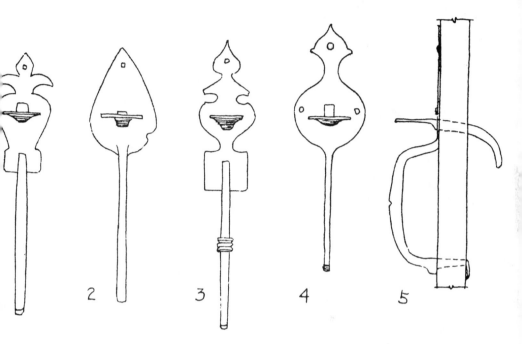

All the old wrought iron French door latches found in the Illinois Country were of this type, called a "single cusp Suffolk latch." They may
well have been imports from continental Europe.

(1) From house demolished 1939, Isle d'Orleans, P.Q. *Coll: author.*
(2) Excavated at Guibourd House, Ste. Genevieve. *Coll: Jules Valle.*
(3) In place at Bequet-Ribault House, Ste. Genevieve.
(4) From Bolduc House, Ste. Genevieve. *Coll: Mrs. Obermueller.*
(5) Section of No. 4 (latchbar and keeper missing).
Drawings by Frank R. Leslie, National Park Service

Casements swinging in on hinges were typical of French buildings generally. Ste. Genevieve's Guibourd House has the only remaining originals in the Illinois Country. The type was superseded by double-hung sash introduced from the East. The house was restored in the 1930s by owner Jules Valle. *Author, 1937.*

This board shutter at the Bequet-Ribault House swings outward. It is held together by a dovetailed and tapered batten in the continental manner. The wrought iron strap hinge, swinging on a pintle driven into the window frame, could be Anglo-American. *Author, 1937.*

Charles E. Peterson, FAIA

Bachrach

Charles E. Peterson is a native of Minnesota and a graduate of the University of Minnesota, where he studied architecture. Early in 1929 he began his professional work at the Western Field Headquarters of the National Park Service in San Francisco. The following year he was assigned to the Eastern Seaboard to plan for several new historical and scenic projects. These included the Colonial National Historical Park, Jamestown to Yorktown, Virginia; the Skyline Drive in the Blue Ridge Mountains; and the Great Smoky Mountains National Park. While on that duty in 1933 he inaugurated the Historic American Buildings Survey (HABS). HABS, administered by the National Park Service, has made more than 46,500 measured drawings and 110,500 large-format photographs of early American buildings. The documents are archived in the Library of Congress.

In June 1936, with the beginning the Jefferson National Expansion Memorial (JNEM) on the downtown St. Louis riverfront, Peterson moved to St. Louis as senior landscape architect. Some of the activities he directed there were the restoration of the Manuel Lisa warehouse at the foot of Chestnut Street (since demolished), the beginning of the rehabilitation of St. Louis's Old Courthouse, the transcription and indexing of the colonial archives, and numerous special studies.

Peterson lectured widely during his stay in St. Louis. He was a founder and secretary of the William Clark Society, president of the St. Louis Historical Documents Foundation, and a member of the board of directors of the Missouri Historical Society.

During World War II Peterson served on the staff of Adm. Chester W. Nimitz at Pearl Harbor. He held the rank of commander and was chief of advanced base engineering in the U.S. Navy's Civil Engineer Corps.

Peterson is a Fellow of the American Institute of Architects and past president of the Society of Architectural Historians. He also served as president of the Association for Preservation Technology.

He retired in 1962 from the National Park Service as supervising architect of historic structures of the Eastern Office of Design and Construction. He is a charter member of the National Trust for Historic Preservation and received its Louise du Pont Crowninshield Award in 1963. He was a member of the Philadelphia Historical Commission, 1956-64; adjunct professor of Architecture at Columbia University, 1964-78; and currently is company historian emeritus of the Carpenters' Company of the city and county of Philadelphia.

Peterson has been widely published. His St. Louis studies on the Mississippi Valley French include:

"A Museum of American Architecture" (proposed for the JNEM), in *The Octagon, Journal of the American Institute of Architects,* 1936;

"French House of the Illinois Country," in *Missouriana,* 1938;

"The Old St. Louis Riverfront," St. Louis, 1938;

"Notes on Old Cahokia," in *French-American Review,* 1938. (In a much enlarged version, this was published in the *Journal of the Illinois State Historical Society* in 1949);

"A List of Published Writings of Special Interest in the Study of Historic Architecture of the Mississippi Valley," JNEM, 1940;

"Old Ste. Genevieve and Its Architecture," in *Missouri Historical Review,* 1941;

"Manuel Lisa's Warehouse," in *Missouri Historical Society Bulletin,* 1948;

"Early French Landmarks Along the Mississippi," in *Antiques,* 1948;

"The Houses of French St. Louis," in *The French in the Mississippi Valley,* John Francis McDermott, Ed., 1965; and "Before the Arch: Architects and Engineers on the St. Louis Riverfront," (in preparation).